BUSHY PARK

Royals, Rangers and Rogues

by

Kathy White and Peter Foster

Cover: *Bushy House*, Turner School, 19th century
Reproduced by kind permission of the Royal Society

First published 1997 by Foundry Press
Clarence Cottage, Hampton Court Road
East Molesey, Surrey KT8 9BY

British Library Cataloguing in Publication Data
A catalogue record for this book is available from the British Library

ISBN 0 9530245 0 4

Typographically Designed, Printed and Bound by B.A.S. Printers Ltd., Stockbridge, Hampshire

Contents

Acknowledgements

The authors are indebted to Dr John Rae, Director,
National Physical Laboratory, for the help and
encouragement generously offered in preparing this book.
Thanks for practical advice and contributions are many and
due especially to Joan Heath, Sue Osborne, Valerie Sullivan,
Dr Charles Avery, Pippa Hyde, the Bushy Park Wildlife Group,
Charles Freeman, Dr Miklós Rajnai, Jane Crawley, Geoffrey Fisher,
James Sullivan and to the Friends of Bushy and Home Parks

Introduction

Bushy Park holds a strange and beautiful enchantment for the thousands of people who visit each year. The influence of kings and statesmen together with the demands of the great social and political upheavals in past years can be traced in the wide open spaces and the tranquillity of Bushy Park today. Henry VIII, Charles I and William IV are all monarchs who have left lasting impressions. The great architect, Sir Christopher Wren, the writers Daniel Defoe and James Boswell, painters such as Thomas Rowlandson and Jacob Bogdani have all worked, written or painted in Bushy.

Today, the park includes the remains, often showing only as ground markings, of the different uses to which the land has been put over the last several thousand years. Delving back through the centuries it is possible to unravel the clues left behind. It is not immediately obvious, for instance, that the reason for the existence of such large areas of bracken in the park is the fall in the price of wool during the Middle Ages. Nor does it spring to mind that Bushy would probably not be a park at all if Richmond Palace had not burned down five hundred years ago, or if Oliver Cromwell had not found the idea of deer hunting in keeping with his position as Protector of the Commonwealth.

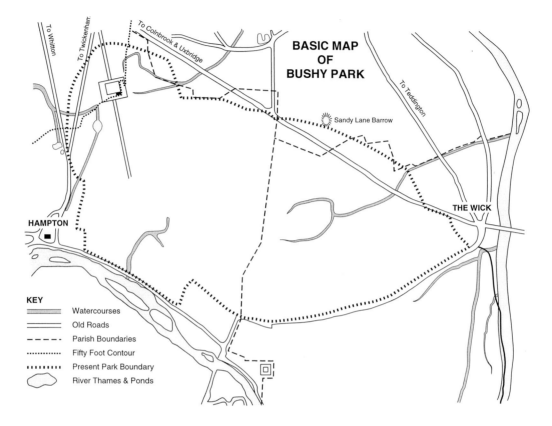

BASIC MAP
OF
BUSHY PARK

To Whitton

To Twickenham

To Colnbrook & Uxbridge

To Teddington

Sandy Lane Barrow

THE WICK

HAMPTON

KEY

Watercourses
Old Roads
Parish Boundaries
Fifty Foot Contour
Present Park Boundary
River Thames & Ponds

MAP I

1. The Origins of Bushy Park

Bushy Park lies close to the Thames and to Hampton Court Palace and is surrounded by the parishes of Hampton, Hampton Hill, Teddington and Hampton Wick. Its acid grasslands are mostly just above the 25 foot contour.

In Tudor times the several enclosures which made up today's park north of the road from Hampton Court to Kingston Bridge were known as North Park, while South Park was the modern Home Park which is attached to Hampton Court Palace.

What must be the oldest visible feature in Bushy Park is a wide, low ridge crossing under the wall into the park from Sandy Lane, Teddington, near the entrance to Shaef Way. It has probably been in existence for some four thousand years.

During the Middle Bronze Age a highly important local man died. He was cremated and two thousand tons of sand were piled on his charred bones to form what came to be called the Sandy Lane Barrow. A little of the edge of the barrow can still be seen in its original position and it is

Fig. 1 *Bronze dagger found during excavation of barrow in 1854. After 4000 years this major landmark was almost entirely destroyed in the 1860s when the railway came to Teddington. There is a strong possibility that the earth from it now forms part of the Broad Lane side of Teddington railway bridge*

obvious that it stood on and was associated with that wide, low ridge.

Part of the layout of the park may well date back to the Romans. There is a set of parallel features, ancient field edges, ditches, fence lines and roads that can clearly be seen to form a rectangular pattern aligned about ten degrees west of north, not only covering almost all of the park but extending far beyond it. The medieval fields in the park conform to this pattern, as do later features based on them.

Significantly, the pattern is not medieval, nor is it modern. It has not arisen by chance, nor has it been forced by the accidental configuration of the land. It was planned. And it was planned before the medieval agriculture there was laid out. It is difficult to avoid the conclusion that we have here a survival from the Romans. Even some of the spacings of the elements of the system seem to be based on the 'actus' which was the Roman surveyor's unit. An actus was a measure of 120 Roman feet, just over 35 metres. Just as one can recognise how medieval field edges outside the park have become modern roads, so one may perhaps be able to work back from the medieval roads and fields still plainly visible in the park to infer an even earlier system.

It is not impossible that surviving minor Roman roads, perhaps to Hampton and the easy crossings of the Thames at Hampton Court and Teddington, could have been kept in use and utilised as boundaries of fields. The major roads in this area certainly were.

There definitely was a local Roman presence. Roman pottery shards have been found at Hampton Wick east of the park, and many accidental finds of Roman material have been made in Hampton and nearby. The ford over the Thames at Kingston must have been important to the Romans as it was one of the few places where it was possible to march men and animals across the river at low tide.

The Romans gave way to other European invaders – the Anglo-Saxons – and Hampton and Teddington were among the early settlements by these Teutonic peoples. The new settlers brought with them the Ridge-and-Furrow system of agriculture which was a radical new approach to land use. Half of the park is covered by ridges or butts which are the remains of this medieval system (see Fig. 3).

The Hounslow Hundred, which included Hampton, Teddington, Twickenham, Whitton and Isleworth, was the property of the kings and earls of Mercia for centuries before the Norman Conquest, although none of them lived there. The last Mercian holder was Aelfgar, earl of Mercia, son of Leofric and the lady Godiva.

It was almost certainly Godiva who granted Teddington to Westminster Abbey. She and Leofric were with Edward the Confessor and shared with him the 'miraculous' vision of a child which led to the founding of the Abbey. Teddington was among the nearest of her possessions to Westminster, and she was an enthusiastic benefactor to religious foundations. She would not have missed a chance like that.

After the Norman invasion the Hounslow Hundred, including Hampton, passed to the family of Walter de St Valery, one of whose descendants sold Hampton to a London merchant, Henry de St Albans. He in turn sold it to the Knights Hospitaller of St John of Jerusalem, a Benedictine military order, in 1237.

The Knights Hospitaller were established in the eleventh century although the first records of the organisation in England came a century later. The order was founded upon the great hospital in Jerusalem. Its original object was to provide accommodation for pilgrims to the Holy Land, although the order was later permitted to undertake military activities which shortly took precedence over its charitable work. After the surrender of Jerusalem to Saladin in 1187 the hospital there was lost and the order became completely military. Its headquarters removed first to Rhodes in 1310, where it remained for the next two hundred years, and then to Malta.

Fig. 2 *The Priory of St John of Jerusalem in Clerkenwell: Headquarters of the Knights Hospitaller in England*

The Hospitallers acquired land and holdings throughout England and as early as 1180 already owned a house on the site of today's Hampton Court Palace which had an enclosed sheep pasture attached to it. The acquisition of the Manor of Hampton brought them more land to manage.

Normally, the lord of the manor, like his tenants, had arable strips scattered separately within the town fields. His serfs worked the land for him as a customary duty. The Hospitallers, though, had no need for farm produce; their compelling need was for money to maintain the headquarters of their order on the island of Rhodes. As a result, they turned to new management methods which would affect the land for ever.

There still survives a financial survey of the Hampton holdings of the Hospitallers which was made in 1338. By then, 40 acres of meadow and 800 acres of arable were rented out and 2000 sheep were kept.

The Hospitallers decided the only way to increase revenue was an efficiency drive. To achieve this, they gathered all their arable land into a large block near their house by means of exchanging strips of land with the villagers or, in some cases, by confiscating them. However, they made a change in the design of the arable they had newly appropriated.

After Britain had entered the 'Little Ice Age' early in this millennium the original arable acres had proved to be too large to plough in a short winter's day. Accordingly the ploughmen had turned them into half-acres by halving their width. The Hospitallers, though, returned the demesne (the land they were renting out), back into full acres. But they did so not by combining the half-acres side by side but instead they set them end to end. The boundaries between two old arable fields were

Fig. 3 *Medieval plough. The plough lifted the earth and threw it to the right. In opening up new land a first cut was made about a furlong (200 metres) long. The plough was then turned right and run back alongside the original furrow, throwing earth back into it. The process was repeated, always turning right and moving outwards, until the plough had gone two rods (10 metres) each side of the first cut. The ridge that was so formed was an acre in area. It was a comfortable day's ploughing for the spring sowing. The ploughmen then moved two rods sideways and started another acre. After they and their descendants had repeated the process for generations these ridges were difficult to erase even when the land was later flat-ploughed*

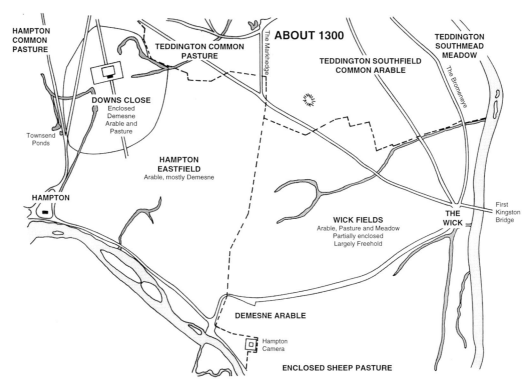

MAP II

ploughed across to form acres two rods (10 metres) wide by a quarter of a mile (400 metres) long; where this could not be done, as in the field south of Upper Lodge, they ploughed along the field instead of across it. These long acres are extremely unusual; indeed Bushy Park may be unique in this respect.

With their holdings closer together the villagers should have been able to till the land more efficiently. A tax assessment of 1340 said the local parishioners 'were so impoverished that their lands could not be sown'. This does not necessarily indicate a poverty level. The wily parishioners had worked out that it was cheaper to rent land from the Hospitallers (who had bought exemption from feudal obligations) than to pay a tenth of their income as a statutory tithe to the parish and as much or more again in tax to the King to pay for his wars.

The Hospitallers' main source of money was the sale of wool from their sheep. Unfortunately, wool was falling in value, and between 1300 and 1500 wool prices halved. So to make up the shortfall, arable land at Hampton Wick was bought and enclosed to run more sheep. This proved to be a disastrous mistake. For over a thousand years, barley had been cultivated as the main grain staple. Barley bread and ale played a major part in the diet of most people. The long history of single crop farming on the land had impoverished it and the practice of running too many sheep on depleted grassland encouraged the growth of bracken. After a few decades of overgrazing, the bracken spread uncontrollably and made the pasture useless. Where today there are large expanses of bracken, as in the eastern part of the park, it is clear that the land was once arable and later a sheep run.

The Hospitallers looked to a radical change of land use in an attempt to solve their financial pressures. They turned to a far more profitable form of livestock; rabbits. These were still a relatively recent import to Britain. The first local warren had been set up on an island in the Thames at Richmond in 1215. Three hundred years later, a breeding stock of 2000 rabbits at Hampton Court produced an income of over £70, which was about five times the sum 2000 sheep would have afforded. The rabbit was a luxury item then; the Hospitallers sold theirs to a London poulterer.

There was a certain amount of confusion in references to rabbits

Fig. 4 *A fourteenth century sheep fold*

and hares; the names often appear interchangeable. The hare is native to Britain and does not live in a warren. It entered the country while Britain was still connected to the mainland of Europe. The rabbit, though, was confined to the Iberian peninsula after the last Ice Age. It was deliberately spread from there during the eleventh and twelfth centuries by the inhabitants of monastic institutions. The rabbit had the great advantage not only that it bred very quickly but that the Church did not define rabbit flesh as meat. It could be eaten on fast days and Fridays.

Fig. 5 *A rabbit warren*

The Hospitallers' house at Hampton Court had been used for many years as emergency overflow accommodation for the Royal palace of Sheene by the river at Richmond. As early as 1353, it is recorded that Edward III had paid for the rebuilding of the Hampton house after his servants accidentally set fire to it one night when he was staying there. But just before Christmas in 1497 an event occurred that led directly to the creation of Bushy Park. Sheene Palace, by then called Richmond Palace, was burnt to the ground.

Building work started immediately to replace the palace and the royal court stayed from time to time at Hampton Court. This was to determine the future of the land of Bushy Park. It became a matter of urgency to entertain the courtiers and, in those times, it was the hunting, shooting and coursing which were the most popular diversions as a means of recreation.

Fig. 6 *Edward III*

Accordingly, in 1500, the Lord Chamberlain, Sir Giles Daubeney, had 300 acres of the demesne arable land of Hampton enclosed. He turned it into a park and stocked it with deer. It was the middle part of the present park, roughly between Chestnut Avenue and the line between the present Woodland Gardens (see MAP III page 15). As a direct result of that enclosure, Bushy Park still contains the best preserved medieval field system in the county of Middlesex.

In 1505, Sir Giles took out a lease of 'there manour of Hampton courte' from the Hospitallers. This time it was for himself rather than the King. When Daubeney died in 1508, he left the lease to his wife. She let it lapse, and in January 1515 the Hospitallers made another lease of the manor; this new lease was to the ambitious Cardinal Wolsey.

Wolsey rebuilt the Hospitallers' house in palatial style. In the 1520s, his power was seen to be a threat to the King and he found it expedient to give Hampton Court to Henry VIII. After the suppression of the Order of the Hospitallers of St John, the Crown annexed it and in 1540 Hampton Court, with other land from Esher to Hounslow Heath, was created as a separate 'honour,' that is, a hunting preserve. Henry was now Lord of the Manor. In 1536 he had acquired Teddington in an exchange of property from the Abbot of Westminster Abbey. Now it was possible to add Teddington land to the park and the boundary on the north side of the park became set in its modern position, using the Sandy Lane Barrow as marker and sighting point to lay out the paling fence to enclose the land (see Map III).

Fig. 7 *King Henry VIII*

The following year saw immense activity within the park. A local bricklayer, Thomas Clement, was employed to build brick walls from Hampton Court to Hampton Wick and another from Hampton Court to Teddington. This was to provide a course or chase where rabbits could be chased along by hounds. Bushy became a favourite for hunting with Henry VIII. Elizabeth I, who was an excellent horsewoman, followed her father's love of the chase.

Fig. 8 *The mark of Thomas Clement. His trademark, included in the walls he was building around Hampton Court and Bushy Park, has now disappeared*

The park also grew in size during this year. An already enclosed area of arable land near Hampton town, around the house now called Upper Lodge, was emparked. Many bushels of acorns were planted south of the house with the idea that they would eventually grow into timber for the successor to Henry VIII's New Navy. It was probably the protective thorny undergrowth planted around these oaks which led to this new park acquiring the name of 'Bushy' Park, which was first recorded in 1604.

Henry wanted to increase the land available for hunting and so made a useless attempt to destroy the 200 acres of bracken near Hampton Wick by mowing it. When this failed, he leased the land out to pay for the maintenance of his warren of black rabbits near the park gate by Hampton Court. By 1565 the black rabbits were gone, probably by interbreeding with the ordinary brown, but the leases continued until the early seventeenth century. When these finally ran out 'a warren for hares' was enclosed there in 1607. From then on,

Fig. 9 *Queen Elizabeth I at a Hunt Picnic. Anonymous woodcut, 1575*

the Hampton Wick part of the the park was known as the Harewarren.

The last enclosure of land to complete Bushy Park was made in 1620. An area known as Hampton Eastfield or Court Field was taken into the Tudor North Park (see MAP IV page 20). So now the North Park consisted of four enclosed sections: the 'Harewarren' near Hampton Wick, the 'Middle Park' or 'Jockey Park', west of that; 'Old Bushy Park', west again and projecting into the heathland north of Hampton; and the new part of 'Bushy Park', the 1620 enclosure, next to Hampton town itself. The boundaries of today's Bushy Park were now complete.

Charles I was responsible for the next major feature of the park. In 1638 he ordered a canal to be cut from the Longford Mills on the Colne River to Hampton Court to supply the palace with extra water.

During the Commonwealth period, Parliament sold off the North Park as being a godless luxury unsuited to the Puritan ideal. Luckily, Oliver Cromwell decided to live at Hampton Court, so the park was hastily bought back at a loss. Without this whim of Cromwell, there would be no Bushy Park today.

Cromwell was also responsible for the digging of the ponds in the Harewarren to stock as fish ponds for sport as well as for the table. Isaak Walton's popular discourse on the pleasures of fishing, *The Compleat Angler,* had just been published. Angling, or fishing with a hook instead of a net, was becoming a fashionable sport. The ponds were originally fed from springs in the park.

The Longford River had been dammed during the Civil War by a mob of local people furious with the nuisance it had caused since its completion by cutting across their roads and by flooding paths. It was not opened

Fig. 10 *The lease of 200 acres in the Harewarren to maintain the warren of black rabbits near Hampton Court Gate 1546*

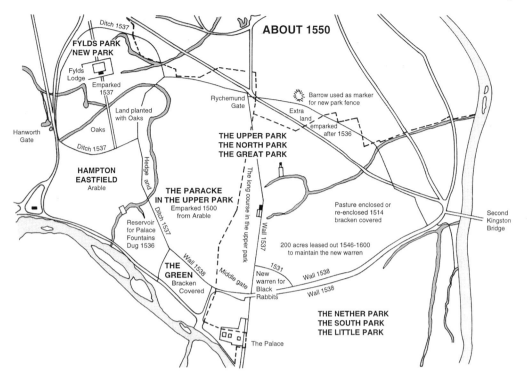

ABOUT 1550

FYLDS PARK
NEW PARK

Fylds
Lodge

Emparked
1537

Ditch 1537

Land planted
with Oaks

Oaks

Hanworth
Gate

Ditch 1537

Rychemund
Gate

Barrow used as marker
for new park fence

Extra
land
emparked
after 1536

THE UPPER PARK
THE NORTH PARK
THE GREAT PARK

HAMPTON
EASTFIELD
Arable

Hedge and

THE PARACKE
IN THE UPPER PARK
Emparked 1500
from Arable

Ditch 1537

Reservoir
for Palace
Fountains
Dug 1536

Wall 1538

The long course in the upper park

Wall 1537

Pasture enclosed or
re-enclosed 1514
bracken covered

Second
Kingston
Bridge

200 acres leased out 1546-1600
to maintain the new warren

THE
GREEN
Bracken
Covered

Middle gate

1531
New
warren for
Black
Rabbits

Wall 1538

Wall 1538

THE NETHER PARK
THE SOUTH PARK
THE LITTLE PARK

The Palace

MAP III

up again until the Restoration of Charles II. However, when it was finally unblocked, the Hampton Manor Court made vociferous complaints that the turning of the Longford water to feed Cromwell's new ponds had flooded the old road across the park from Hampton Wick to Teddington.

To replace the old deer course in South Park (Home Park), a series of paddocks and a new course were made in North Park along the road to Kingston. The deer were loosed at the Hampton Wick end and chased by dogs as far as a stand near the present Hampton Court Gate. This course has gone but the paddocks remain.

William III decided to rebuild Hampton Court Palace in the 1690s in consultation with Sir Christopher Wren in his position as Surveyor of the Fabric. Wren defined a ceremonial approach to the north side of the new palace. The rebuilding of the palace was never completed.

When riding in the parks one day, William's horse stumbled on a molehill, mortally injuring his master. The humble mole, who inadvertently had been the cause of the downfall of the arch enemy to

Fig. 11 *Woodcut of an angler 1496*

the cause of Scottish succession to the throne, was commemorated by the Jacobites with a toast: 'To the little gentleman in velvet'. It is ironical that the horse, Sorrel, which threw William to the ground, had been confiscated from the estate of Sir John Fenwick, a Jacobite conspirator who had been unjustly executed for treason on a trumped-up charge; a posthumous revenge for Fenwick which must have delighted the Jacobites.

Mole

Each of the divisions of the North Park had its own under-keeper for managing the game and also its own keeper's lodge. These keeperships became sinecures and by the early eighteenth century two of the lodges had become magnificent country houses for their holders. The lodge in the Middle Park, now known as Bushy House, cost the sum of four thousand pounds to construct in the 1660s, which is equivalent to around half a million pounds today. In writing of his visit in 1724, Daniel Defoe was so impressed that he described it as almost a palace in its own right.

The other grand house was the keeper's lodge for Old Bushy Park. The Earl of Halifax took down the old wooden lodge there, which had been crippled by the great storm of 1703, and rebuilt it into a very similar house to the one in the Middle Park, though rather smaller. It came to be called the 'Upper Lodge'.

The fence between the Middle Park and Old Bushy Park was removed and over the next century the name of Bushy Park spread to include the whole of the North Park. This trend was encouraged by the replacement in 1737 of the fence round the north side of the park from Hampton to Hampton Wick by a brick wall, so turning an assemblage of separate enclosures into a visible unity.

The next great change came when the Duke of Clarence, later William IV, became Keeper of Bushy Park in 1797. He had ambitions as a gentleman farmer and treated Bushy as his personal estate in an effort to improve his finances.

He enclosed over half the park into pasture and arable, leaving little more than 500 acres as parkland. The last of the Tudor timber oaks were felled and sold, leaving Bushy almost denuded of trees. To give the Duke of Clarence his due, he then instituted new planting. Most of the present oak stands date from his time. They were planted for the Navy and would normally have been felled about a century ago, but by that time Britain no longer needed oak to build wooden warships.

English Oak

The Duke of Clarence became King in 1830 and left Bushy; his intrusive fences were removed, leaving the park much as it is today. The mid-nineteenth century saw a little more tree planting and a few changes in fence lines. At the same time, the park slowly turned into a playground for the people. Londoners came down for hare coursing meetings there, and to see the chestnut trees in bloom in May. Chestnut Sunday became a traditional day out to admire the blooms.

The twentieth century saw more changes, but most were only temporary. One of the more permanent was the use of Bushy House as the nucleus of the new National Physical Laboratory in 1900.

When General Eisenhower needed a headquarters for the Allied Expeditionary Force, he located it in the Teddington part of Bushy Park. His hut camp covered over 50 acres. Another camp was set up near Hampton Hill. After the war, these camps were dismantled and the land returned to the park.

Upper Lodge had been requisitioned at the start of hostilities and accommodated Americans from the United States Army Air Force. It was later used by the Admiralty Research Laboratory. The lease has now expired and the laboratory has moved out.

A number of trees have been lost over the last few years. An earlier gale in 1908 took its toll and the hurricanes of 1978 and 1987 knocked down many more. Some of the finest trees succumbed to Dutch Elm Disease.

Today, Bushy Park is now almost entirely open to the public by order of Queen Victoria. Deer still roam but are no longer hunted or coursed and rabbits are a nuisance rather than an asset. Sheep are long gone, although cattle were pastured in Bushy until the end of the 1970s. A large area is devoted to the playing of games and the old oak stands have been transformed into pleasure gardens It is now many a year since there were any hares in Harewarren. Although no longer worked or farmed, Bushy Park still retains a remarkable air of quiet rural charm.

2. Upper Lodge

Upper Lodge is without doubt the oldest of the occupied sites in Bushy Park. It is surrounded by medieval Ridge-and-Furrow ploughing which is so well integrated and aligned with the lodge itself that the two must either be contemporary or, far more likely, the lodge was already there when the land around it was ploughed.

There is a strong possibility that Upper Lodge started its existence as a small Roman marching fort, standing just where the land starts to drop away to the Thames and commanding the bend of the river from Teddington to Hampton, together with the great ford at Kingston. When the Anglo-Saxons arrived they could well have continued to use the site, perhaps as their manor house for Hampton, and then laid out their ploughland around it.

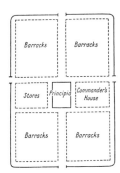

Fig. 12 *Diagram of a typical Roman fort*

The lodge is aligned with the set of parallel features, ten degrees west of north, that cover the park and extend well beyond it. This configuration is far too elaborate and exact to be medieval and parts of it can be shown to have forced the layout of the medieval arable. A Roman fort was shaped like a playing card, divided into three sections, with a road running through it bisecting the long sides (see Fig.12). That is still a fairly good description of the Upper Lodge site. The road can be seen as a ridge running from the park wall to the north gate of the lodge and continuing south of it to the Waterhouse Woodland Gardens.

Upper Lodge was certainly there in 1537 when the land around it, then arable, was added to the Tudor North Park. It was already occupied by one John Field (also, Feld/Fyld) and for a while the new park was called 'Fyld's Park'.

The Keeper of Hampton Court Palace and Chief Steward of the Honour of Hampton was also keeper of all the parks there; he appointed an under-keeper for each. The egregious George Villiers, Duke of Buckingham, was made Steward of the Honour in 1616, and he assigned John Hippesley to be under-keeper of Bushy Park with Upper Lodge as his local residence.

Hippesley was an opportunist, always on the look-out for an advantage. In 1605 he had been examined about the Gunpowder Plot. He was suspected of having arranged the lease of the London house in which the gunpowder was stored before being moved to the Houses of Parliament to arch-plotter Thomas Percy. Hippesley is mentioned in a further enquiry in 1611, but nothing more was done. By then he was Governor of Dover Castle.

It is almost certain that Hippesley was a member of the syndicate, organised by the Archbishop of Canterbury, George Abbot, which promoted and financed George Villiers in his successful attempt to seduce the homosexual James I. Villiers's progress in court circles was phenomenally fast and his cronies benefited accordingly; when Villiers was made an earl in 1617, Hippesley was knighted.

There were obligations as well as advantages, however. Villiers's elder brother, Viscount Purbeck, became insane and had to be kept out of the public eye. In 1623 Sir John Hippesley was told to take Purbeck into his charge; a few days later he wrote, saying he had brought Purbeck to Hampton Court without noise and had done all he could to avoid scandal, but prayed 'to be freed from further concern in that business'.

Villiers was assassinated in 1628; it was Hippesley who had the difficult task of breaking the news to Charles I. Charles doted on Villiers as much as James I had done.

Sir John continued his lucrative career; he became a Member of Parliament and engaged in various speculations. He was given letters of marque in 1629 which gave him licence to fit out and arm a vessel with which to capture enemy merchant shipping. He was briefly arrested two years later for appropriating 500 French crowns from a vessel taken as a prize. The petitioner for the return of his money was warned to have a care, for 'Sir John is the King's servant'.

Sir John also became one of the commissioners for the new canal cut from Longford to Hampton Court in 1638. During the Civil War he exchanged the uncertainties of a courtier's life to become a supporter of Parliament and in 1648 he guarded the ferries at Hampton and Hampton Court against the Royalists.

In 1653 an inventory of the parks was made preparatory to selling them. Upper Lodge was described as 'the messuage or dwelling house in the tenure of Sir John Hippesley, commonly called the Greater Lodge, consisting of a hall, a faire parlor, a kitchen, a pantry, and other convenient Roomes belowe stayres, seven Lodging roomes above stayres, with a Large Barne, Stable, and other outhouses, belonging to the same'. The materials of the Lodge were worth £159.10s.8d. The trees in that part of the park were valued at £620.6s.8d. Since mature oaks are quoted elsewhere in the inventory at ten shillings each, there must have been about 1200 oaks still left of the Tudor planting. 'Bushie Park' then included not only the 183 acres round Upper Lodge, known as the Old Park, but also 167 acres south of that, emparked in 1620.

There is a local tradition that Upper Lodge was occupied for a while by John Bradshaw, the president of the court that condemned Charles I to death. It may not be true; but certainly Parliament had given another of

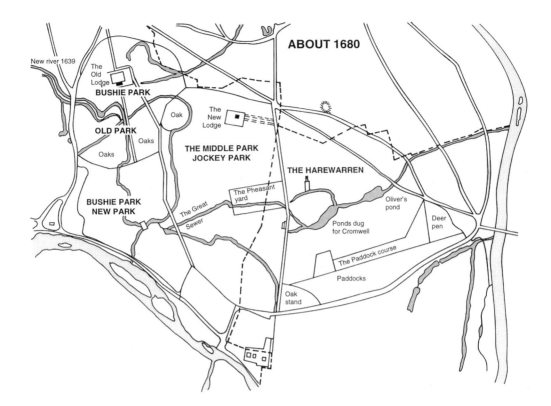

MAP IV

Hippesley's houses, Freemantle Park in Hampshire, to Bradshaw about the same time. Hippesley was by then in debt to Parliament. He died at Richmond.

After the Restoration the keepership of Bushy Park was given to Silius Titus, a friend and supporter of the new King. He, like Hippesley, had been a turncoat, though the other way round. He was a captain in Cromwell's army and was voted £50 by Parliament for bringing the news of the King's capture in 1647.

The King escaped from Hampton Court Palace and when he was recaptured and imprisoned at Carisbrooke Castle, Titus had himself appointed as attendant on the King's person. By then he was a secret Royalist and began plotting with the King to organise another escape. There still exist letters from the King to him about the details.

Cromwell suspected Titus's loyalty, however, and had him removed. Shortly afterwards he was accused of high treason and fled to France. On the scaffold, the King recommended Titus to the protection of his son, Charles II.

Titus returned to England secretly at least twenty times to organise resistance to the Commonwealth. On one occasion, in 1651, Cromwell heard that he and another Royalist, Henry Firebrace, were at the King's Arms Inn in Holborn, London.

The officer sent to arrest them confirmed with the innkeeper that they were there, then wrapped his red cloak round his head, entered the room where the plotters were and cried, 'If Titus or Firebrace are in this room, let them escape for their lives this instant', then retired to fetch his soldiers. When he came back Titus had climbed out through the window and escaped, leaving behind him a horse and a 'study of books'.

By July he was with 'the King of Scotland' (Charles II) in Scotland. In May 1658 he was back in England; the Council of State ordered him to be seized and examined. He was popularly, but wrongly, supposed to be the author of a scurrilous pamphlet called *Killing No Murder*, recommending Cromwell's assassination.

After the Restoration, Titus received his well-earned reward. Honours and money were heaped upon him; he was made a Groom of the King's Bedchamber, Governor of Deal Castle and given the sinecure of keeper of Bushy Park. Parliament voted him £3000 for his services and for introducing a motion that the bodies of Cromwell, Ireton and John Bradshaw be disinterred from Westminster Abbey, hanged at Tyburn, and their heads set upon Westminster Hall; this grisly proposal was indeed carried out.

Titus did live at Upper Lodge for a while, but when his father died in 1667 he retired to his father's mansion at Bushey in Hertfordshire. He stayed active in politics, objecting strongly to the succession of James II to the throne; nevertheless James made him a member of his Privy Council. He died in 1704 and was buried in Bushey parish church in Hertfordshire.

Meanwhile, John Lightfoot had been granted the custody of Bushy Park. From 1667 to about 1680 Lightfoot was resident at Upper Lodge and rather more active about the park than most of the Keepers. He requested authority to prosecute 'persons who have stolen or sold deer out of the park'. He obtained convictions for some but was unable to catch all the poachers.

By 1684 he was dead and his son, who apparently had a right to the keepership of Bushy Park, had disappeared somewhere in the West Indies. Henry Savile, the brother of George Savile, Marquess of Halifax, was made keeper, having spent much money trying to prove that Lightfoot's son was dead and that the keepership was vacant.

Henry was a courtier, a protégé of the Duke of York and, like Titus, a Groom of the Bedchamber to Charles II. He became Envoy to Paris, Commissioner to the Admiralty and Vice Chamberlain. He was also notorious as a drunkard and as a friend of John Wilmot, Earl of Rochester, poet and libertine.

In December 1685 he petitioned the Treasury for money to bring the lodge and park up to standard, complaining that they were in severe disorder. The paling around Bushy Park and between it and the Middle Park needed replacing. The lodge was very old and almost past repair. A brick wall round the garden would cost £250, though to rebuild the lodge itself was estimated at only £150. The brick wall is still there, the oldest visible survival on the site. Savile also recommended that the land north of the lodge should be ploughed and sown for three years to destroy the rabbits which infested it, to which the Treasury agreed. Before this was finished, Henry Savile was dead.

The next recorded occupant of the lodge was Fitton Gerard, third and last Earl of Macclesfield. In 1700 an avenue of 110 large elms was planted leading to 'my Lord Macclesfield's' from the south, along the line of the old (possibly Roman) road through the lodge grounds. About 2000 tons of earth were moved to make a new garden south of the lodge. Macclesfield died in 1701, and the lodge stayed empty.

When Charles Montagu, Lord Halifax, bought the keepership of Bushy Park early in 1709 he pointed out that the lodge there had been uninhabited for years and was very rotten. It had been crippled by the great storm

of November 1703 and could not be repaired but must be demolished and rebuilt at a cost of £580. He suggested, though, that he might have a 'term therein' to encourage him to rebuild the lodge at his own expense; in other words the lodge should no longer automatically go with the keepership of Bushy Park but would be leased to him personally. The Treasury agreed.

Fig. 13 *Charles Montagu, Earl of Halifax*

In the same year William Young, who had been trustee for the Duchess of Cleveland as head keeper of all the Hampton Court parks since 1677, conveniently died. An ex-mistress of Charles II, the promiscuous Duchess was another member of the ambitious Villiers family. Her son by the King, Henry, Duke of Grafton, had been Keeper of Bushy Park but had never occupied the lodge. On 3 June 1709, Halifax was granted all the Duchess's keeperships at Hampton Court together with other similar offices. These included the reversion of the keepership of Middle Park and Harewarren.

Charles Montagu was a career politician and a Treasury Lord by 1692. He secured Parliamentary approval for the Charter to create the joint stock company which was to become the Bank of England in 1694. It marked the beginning of the funded national debt. He was finally appointed Chancellor of the Exchequer. It was at his instigation that the old silver coinage was called in and reissued as milled money by the Royal Mint, under the Mastership of his great friend, Isaac Newton.

Charles Montagu possessed strong administrative and business abilities. However, his ambition was great as was his vanity and the arrogance of his manner made him many enemies. He narrowly avoided impeachment for dubious political manoeuvrings and gained the reputation of a scoundrel. He fell out of political favour when the Whigs lost power which allowed him time to devote to the creation of his famous house and water gardens and he was made first Baron and then Earl of Halifax.

The house he then built was a slightly smaller copy of the one that had been erected thirty years earlier in the Middle Park. It was not quite on the site of the previous lodge. Halifax's house looked southwards straight along the avenue of elms that had been laid out ten years before for Lord Macclesfield.

Halifax had other improvements made, too. The Longford River had originally run past the lodge to feed the round pond to the south of it, and the old reservoir by the Waterhouse. Halifax diverted the river into a new high pond by the lodge which fed a cascade down to a second pond before discharging to the original system. He presented this idea as an 'improvement of the works that supply water to Her Majesty's gardens'. It had cost him over £1000 to rebuild the lodge and the garden walls, build a brewhouse (still to be seen in the Hampton Hill allotments) and plant the orchard and gardens.

The new ponds were also part of his own ornamental water garden at the lodge. There was a third pond in front of the house itself and Halifax ingeniously also enlarged and aligned with his works the stream arising from a spring east of the lodge, which went through the park fence to Teddington Common.

The water garden was later described by the prolific garden designer and writer, Stephen Switzer, as so famous that it needed no description, but of 'so rude and rustick a manner that it may well serve as a Pattern or Model to any that shall be disposed to make use of Water-Works'.

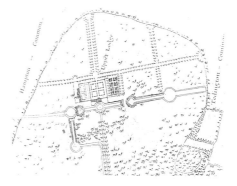

There exists a painting by Jacob Bogdani showing the ponds as they were in the early eighteenth century (see Fig. 16). The identification of the water gardens in this painting as those of Halifax was made only in 1995, when garden historian, Jane Crawley, noticed the sim-

Fig. 14 *Map of the Earl of Halifax's Water Gardens*

ilarity of a catalogue plate of the painting with an engraving already known to be of Upper Lodge (see Fig 15). This was verified by Dr Miklós Rajnai, art historian and leading authority on the paintings of Jacob Bogdani.

The discovery that the backgrounds in Bogdani's paintings could be a faithful rendering of country estates and not merely backdrops to his compositions of exotic birds and fruit has led to a deeper understanding of the work of the painter.

Fig 15 *Eighteenth century engraving of the Water Gardens, Upper Lodge*

In 1729 the water garden was still well known. Stephen Switzer wrote, '. . . the Canal and Cascade at Bushy Park . . . is, without doubt, one of the best works of that kind in England, and perhaps as good as any else where.'

The upper ponds and the cascade survive today and are one of the few baroque water gardens which remain in the Greater London area. Pressure is growing to restore them to their full splendour for all to enjoy.

Halifax was proud of the creation of his gardens. He invited Dean Swift to visit him there; but Swift declined. Writing in his *Journal to Stella* in 1710, he complains, 'Lord Halifax is always teasing me to go down to his country house, which will cost me a guinea to his servants, and twelve shillings coach hire; and he shall be hanged first.'

As one of a circle of men of letters which included Dryden, Addison, Congreve and Garth, Halifax wrote verse himself. He was one of the first patrons of Alexander Pope who was later to move to nearby Twickenham.

On one memorable occasion, the young Pope was reading part of his translation of the *Iliad* to the gathering of Halifax and his literary friends when he was criticised by the Earl who suggested improvements could be made. In some confusion, Pope sought advice from Dr Garth and was told to forget any alterations but to be sure to read the verse again at a later day to the Earl. And indeed, when the same verse was read to him some three months hence, the Earl exclaimed, 'Ay, now they are perfectly right; nothing can be better!'

Halifax died suddenly in 1715. He had first met Isaac Newton at Cambridge and after his wife died he became close to Newton's niece, Catharine Barton. The basis of their relationship was a cause for rumour that they were secretly married or that she was his mistress. In his will, he left Upper Lodge and the keepership of Bushy Park to Catharine, together with bequests of jewels and legacies as a 'token of the sincere Love, Affection and Esteem . . . and as a small recompence for the Pleasure and

Fig. 16 *A pair of peafowl in a park by an ornamental pond, Jacob Bogdani (1660-1724). In the background an be seen the Water Gardens of Upper Lodge together with the Brewhouse*

Fig. 17 *Boys from the King's Canadian School in a pool at Upper Lodge*

Fig. 18 *Pools with cascade at Upper Lodge today*

Happiness I have had in her Conversation'. The keepership was not his to give as it was automatically passed to his heir.

Catharine married two years later, and she and her husband, John Conduitt, probably occupied the lodge occasionally until her death in 1739. Conduitt was to succeed Sir Isaac Newton as Master of the Mint and is buried close to him in Westminster Abbey.

The head keepership of the Hampton Court parks went to Halifax's nephew, George Montagu, first Earl of Halifax of the second creation. He never lived at Upper Lodge; the far grander Bushy House in Middle Park was more his style.

Who inhabited Upper Lodge after Catharine Barton died is unrecorded. By 1823 the house was still square as Halifax had built it, although a bay had been added to the south front. The present yellow-brick house must have been built by 1840 when it was a Grace and Favour residence occupied by the Earl of Denbigh. It has been suggested that it was designed by Sir John Soane.

Upper Lodge continued as Grace and Favour in the Queen's gift throughout the nineteenth century. In 1854 it was occupied by Lady Isabella Wemyss, widow of General Wemyss, Equerry to the Queen. After she died in 1868 it was given to Lord Alfred Paget, Equerry and Clerk-Marshal of the Royal Household.

He made himself unpopular locally by attempting to exclude the inhabitants of Hampton Hill from the park near Upper Lodge by refusing access through a gate. The gates there had been closed in the mid-eighteenth century, shortly after the present brick wall was built, long before the parish of Hampton Hill was founded.

In 1883 local agitation led to the reopening of the gate at Hampton Hill, much to Paget's disgust. He died in 1888, but his widow continued using Upper Lodge as one of her houses for another twenty-five years. She gave it up in 1913 shortly before her death and it was offered first to Lord Carrington and later to Lord Lincolnshire, both of whom accepted but neither actually came into occupation.

Fig. 19 *The Lodge 1775. The earliest surviving engraving of Upper Lodge*

The clamour of the local population for improved access to the park had started early in Victoria's reign. The opening of the gate from Hampton Hill was soon followed by a new gate from South Teddington.

The importance of this occasion was celebrated with gaily coloured bunting and bands played as local schoolchildren paraded. Then, as now, local people valued Bushy Park as an integral part of their lives. Today there are fourteen gates for pedestrians around the park.

In 1889 a deputation of local dignitaries travelled to Whitehall with a proposal to open a carriageway from the Kingston Bridge end of the park and backed it with the plea that 'if the poorer classes could easily obtain access to . . . Bushy Park, infinite benefit would be conferred upon them. Many would be enabled to withstand the temptations of the public house.'

The Government representative hastily replied to this slightly unrealistic argument that he was 'anxious to make the Royal Parks as much as possible available for the enjoyment of all persons who would take advantage of them'. A statement of admirable pertinacity which is as valid today as it was a hundred years ago.

When the First World War began the Lodge was used to accommodate soldiers' wives and families. It was then loaned to the Canadian Red Cross Society as a hospital and convalescent home for wounded Canadian soldiers.

After the end of the war the King granted Upper Lodge to the London County Council as a holiday 'open air' school for poor boys from the East End of London who were suffering from respiratory diseases. It was known as the King's Canadian School. The soldiers' wards became dormitories and the water gardens, designed by the Earl of Halifax over two centuries previously, provided swimming pools. About 3500 boys a year stayed there which was a successful logistical exercise for the LCC.

At the outbreak of the Second World War, Upper Lodge was requisitioned by the Air Ministry. In June 1941 the United States Eighth Army Air Force arrived to set up camp in Bushy Park and Upper Lodge was designated as a barracks for enlisted men. In the latter part of 1944 chemical warfare experiments were made there.

The requisition for Upper Lodge was transferred from the Air Ministry to the Admiralty in December 1945, for its use as an extension to the Admiralty Research Laboratory at Teddington. A conversion of the requisition into a lease was made retrospectively in 1948. For nearly fifty years, the Admiralty continued in occupation until the Ministry of Defence finally relinquished the lease in 1994. The Crown Estate is now responsible for this historic site and its future is still undecided in detail.

3. Bushy House

Bushy House was the Keeper's lodge for the central part of the North Park. This central part was known as Middle Park and sometimes Jockey Park (see MAP IV). Its present site is a relatively late one. It has no relationship with the medieval features of the park and has been laid out parallel to the park boundary nearby. The Pheasantry, half-way along Chestnut Avenue, which is aligned with ancient arable, was probably the site of the original lodge (see MAP IV).

Pheasants were bred at Hampton Court Palace, possibly from Wolsey's time. At that time, they were kept partly in the dry moat of the palace. By the middle of the seventeenth century they had been moved to Middle Park.

Fig. 20 *Edward Proger*

The first building on the Bushy House site was possibly a stand for spectators to watch rabbit coursing. A warren for black rabbits had been created near the Hampton Court Gate in 1531 and the 'sport' of coursing involved dogs chasing the rabbits along the wall that divided the Middle Park from the Harewarren. Spectators would be positioned on raised ground near the end of the wall. At this point they could place wagers on which dog would outrun the others while chasing the terrified rabbits and often catching those which failed to reach the sanctuary at the end of the course.

A lodge was erected by William May in 1611 for £45 in Middle Park and nine years later, John Rutledge, former Keeper, was granted £100 for 'repairs' to it, although such a sum indicates much rebuilding took place. Four years after these repairs, in 1628, Richard Graham or Grimes was Keeper. He was a protégé of the Duke of Buckingham as was his neighbour at Upper Lodge, Sir John Hippesley.

Within the next twenty years, a new keeper's lodge was built. Under the Commonwealth, this lodge was occupied by James Challenor, a crony of Cromwell. The parliamentary survey of 1653 described 'a large dwelling house or lodge' with outbuildings where Bushy House now stands. Its materials were worth £184 15s., rather more than the Upper Lodge building in Bushy Park, although that was then called the 'Greater Lodge'. Challenor, who was probably the brother of Thomas Challenor, the regicide, disappeared with the Restoration of Charles II.

In 1663 Edward Proger, another of the Grooms of the King's Bedchamber, was commanded by the King to 'build a Lodge for our Service in one of Our Parks att Hampton Court called North Parke'. The lodge he built was magnificent by any standards and was designed by William Samwell, one of Charles II's court architects. It cost four thousand pounds to build; four times more than the Earl of Halifax was to spend on Upper Lodge over forty years later. Proger's house is the nucleus of the present building, although only the embellished plaster moulding on the ceiling of one small room remains visible. The original building has been encased in later brick.

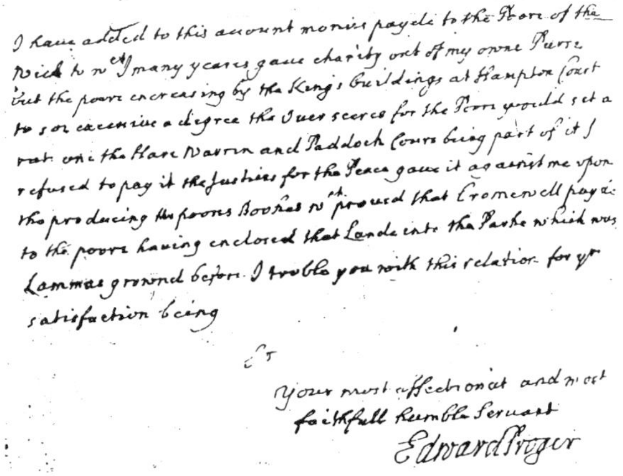
I have added to this account monies payde to the Poore of the
which to wch I many yeares gave charity out of my owne Purse
but the poore encreasing by the Kings Buildings at Hampton Court
to soe excessive a degree the Overseers for the Poore would set a
rate one the Hare Warren and Paddock Course being part of it I
refused to pay it the Justices for the Peace gave it against me upon
the producing the poores Bookes wch proved that Cromewell payde
to the poore having enclosed that Lande into the Parke which was
Lammas grownd before. I trouble you with this relation for yr
satisfaction being

&c

Your most affectionat and most
faithfull humble Servant
Edward Proger

Fig. 21 *Extract from letter by Edward Proger dated 1702. One of the many anxious requests he made for the payment he had been promised*

Edward Proger was the son of a Welsh courtier. He had been a Page of Honour to Charles I and had distinguished himself fighting for the Royalist cause. Charles I commended him to the protection of his son and Proger followed the young prince into poverty and exile, first to Scotland where the Covenanters took offence against him and insisted that he be banished from the court as an 'evil instrument and bad counsellor' of the prince and then to France. Proger, together with other courtiers similarly excluded, had probably objected to Charles having been forced to sign the oath of Covenant before he could be crowned as King of Scotland.

Charles II rewarded his loyalty after the Restoration with money, privilege and offices. They were also personal friends; Proger acted as go-between in the King's dalliances with his many mistresses and it has been suggested that Bushy House was built specifically as a rendezvous for them. It was certainly far too grand for a keeper's lodge.

Andrew Marvell, in one of his satires of the court, *'The Last Instructions to a Painter'* (1667), wrote describing an imaginary procession of courtiers:

> Then the procurers under Progers filed,
> Gentlest of men, and his lieutenant mild,
> Brouncker, Love's squire: through all the field arrayed,
> No troop was better clad nor so well paid.

Henry Brouncker was procurer to the Duke of York, later James II. Proger's wife was one of the King's discarded mistresses and her eldest daughter was said, probably wrongly, to resemble Charles.

It should not be thought that Proger was nothing but a hanger-on; he had become rich and successful in his own right on his return from exile. He was a Member of Parliament, Lord of the Manor of West Stow in Suffolk and owned several houses in London. In his diaries, Samuel Pepys referred to his meetings with Edward Proger. As a member of the navy office, Pepys made occasional visits to Bushy Park to assess the suitability of oaks for use in naval shipping. When Charles II died, however, Proger retired to Bushy House. He had been made Keeper of the Middle Park and Harewarren in November 1665 and remained so for forty-eight years until his death at the age of ninety-two of 'the anguish of cutting teeth'. It is possible that the 'anguish' was caused by an infected late wisdom tooth. He died at Bushy House on New Year's Eve in 1713, and is buried in Hampton parish church. According to the legend on his tomb slab, his kindness and consideration for others, unusual in a courtier, were locally famous. He took his duties as Keeper seriously, and a great deal of information about the parks can be found in his petitions to the Treasury for maintenance payments for their upkeep.

Fig. 22 *Bushy House. Engraving c. 1825*

Proger was never reimbursed by the Treasury for building Bushy House in spite of increasingly desperate pleas for payment over the years. After some forty years, the Treasury cannily agreed to pay him the money as a pension at four hundred pounds a year. He must have felt exasperated by the arrangement, as he was by then ninety years old and was to collect only two instalments.

Edward Proger's death had been impatiently awaited. Charles Montagu, Earl of Halifax and Keeper of Bushy Park, who had purchased the reversion of the keeperships of the Middle Park and Harewarren in 1709, still kept Upper Lodge as his country residence and did not move to Bushy House. In fact, Halifax himself died unexpectedly less than two years after Proger.

The nephew of Halifax, George Montagu, was created Earl of Halifax on a different grant and given the keeperships of Bushy Park, Middle Park and the Harewarren. George was to be encouraged to finish at his

own expense the several works left unfinished by the first Earl in beauti-
fying the parks and rebuilding and repairing the lodges there. Hawthorn
Lodge, to the east of Chestnut Avenue, was one of these. Originally built
as a keeper's lodge for the Harewarren, it appears to have been occupied
by under-keepers. By the middle of the eighteenth century it was a substantial house set in an enclosed garden (see Maps III – V).

By 1850 it had become derelict and it was recommended that it be
pulled down when its occupants, who were pages to Queen Victoria, had
moved elsewhere. The present lodge was rebuilt on the site.

George Montagu had a great interest in all aspects of gardening and re-
designed the gardens to great acclaim. It was during his time that the
present wall round the North Park from Hampton to the Wick was built.

The distinction between the three parks was disappearing now that all
three keeperships were held by the same man. The Tudor wall which
separated the Middle Park and the Harewarren had been demolished
when Chestnut Avenue was laid out about 1700 and the fence between
Bushy Park and the Middle Park disappeared about the same time. Over
a generation or so, the name Bushy Park came to be applied to the whole
of the old North Park.

The house of Edward Proger had been a square block with the main
entrance on the east. By the time George Montagu died in 1737, four
wings had been added, one at each corner, connected with the main block
by curved corridors.

Writing in 1724 in his book *Tour Through the Whole Island of Great Britain*,
Daniel Defoe was exceedingly impressed with the improvements and
said Lord Halifax's house at Bushy Park was one of those near London
which 'wou'd pass for Palaces'. It was surrounded by formal gardens;
also extra land to the east and west had been enclosed out of the park and
added to the already extensive grounds.

George Montagu spent several months each year at Bushy, although his
family estates were at Horton in Northamptonshire. He involved himself
in parish affairs and became a trustee of the local grammar school. He also
persuaded George I to donate £500 to enlarging the Parish Church of
Hampton while making his own donation of £21.

The courtier and diarist, the Earl of Egmont, summed up George
Montagu by confiding to his diary that he was 'a squanderer of his money
so that it is said his daughters will have very small fortune. He was a great
improver of ground, a good companion, loved horse racing and kept a
mistress.' Almost the same could have been said about his son (also
George), the next Earl of Halifax and the next Keeper of the Parks.

Like his great-uncle, the first Earl, George was a successful politician;
among other offices he became First Lord of the Admiralty, head of the

Board of Trade and Lieutenant General of Ireland. Halifax in Nova Scotia is named after him. He married a young heiress whose parents wanted their name preserved, and to oblige them he changed his surname to Montagu Dunk.

After George's wife died, he built Hampton Court House on land enclosed from Hampton Court Green and installed his mistress, the actress, Mary Anne Faulkner, there. Their liaison was much talked about and *The genuine Memoires of Miss Faulkner, Mistress of the Earl of Halifax etc.* was published in 1770, a year before the death of Montagu Dunk. Over a hundred years later, a letter from the Office of Works to the Treasury Solicitor pointed out that the original grant of land from the Crown had been just over three acres, although the house and gardens now covered a total of over eight acres 'showing a considerable portion of Hampton Court Green had afterwards been added'.

Fig. 23 *George Montagu Dunk*

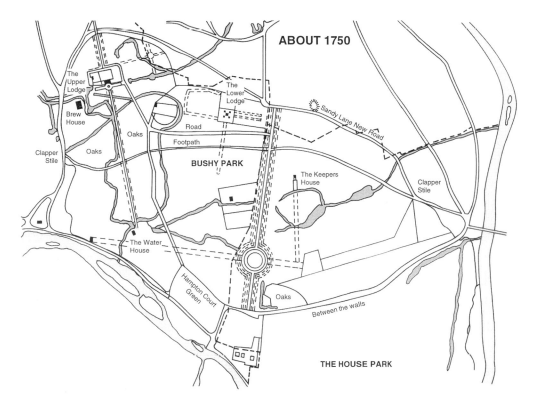

MAP V

With the death of Montagu Dunk, the presentation of the office of Keeper, by then called Ranger, of the three parks reverted to the monarch. George III wished to appoint his prime minister, Lord North, to the post of Ranger but as Members of Parliament were forbidden to hold offices of profit under the Crown it was given to his wife instead. By then, Bushy House was accepted as the Ranger's lodge for all the parks.

Lord North was the grandson of the second Halifax and a cousin of Montagu Dunk. He had probably known Bushy House since he was a child. Now he was happy to use it as his summer residence. There he entertained local luminaries as well as his political allies. The actor, David Garrick of Hampton and Horace Walpole of Strawberry Hill were frequent visitors.

Lord North had become Chancellor of the Exchequer and Leader of the House of Commons in 1767, and First Lord of the Treasury in 1770. He is mainly remembered for his lack of direction in the American War of Independence which resulted in the loss of America as a British colony. The outcry against him was too much to sustain and he resigned his post in 1782, and moved his family to Bushy House.

The Pheasantry enclosure no longer held pheasants and one of Lord North's married daughters, Lady Catherine Douglas, was allowed to refurbish and enlarge a vacant keeper's lodge there into a substantial villa. Repairs were estimated at £1555.12s.6d. and in order to make savings, the paling around the Pheasantry was made an open fence instead of the closed one which had been necessary when pheasants were kept there. This lodge fell into disrepair in the next century and a year before his death, William IV gave orders for it to be pulled down.

It was during this time that the old formal gardens of Bushy House were changed to the newly fashionable, more romantic style of English landscape gardening which remains to this day. There is a tradition that Capability Brown laid them out; it is certainly possible, for Brown was head gardener at Hampton Court at the time and a friend of Lord North.

Two large oaks and a third decayed oak stump south of the house are much older than the present garden. The mounds they stand upon are the original ground level; the lawn has been scooped out into a shallow saucer shape to make it look larger from the house. The ancient Spanish Chestnut near the house is said to have been planted by Charles II. If this garden-loving king actually planted all the trees attributed to him, he certainly made a significant contribution to aboriculture in the land. Actually, with his strong friendship with Edward Proger, it would seem that a regal planting of the Spanish Chestnut is possible in this instance; the tree is certainly of the right age.

Lord North succeeded his father as Earl of Guildford and joined the House of Lords in 1790. By the time of his death two years later, he was blind

and infirm. In his *Life of Dr Johnson* Boswell quotes the Doctor's short opinion of Lord North. The lexicographer's comment was terse and succinct. 'He
fills a chair' was the Doctor's opinion. At one time, Dr Johnson had applied
for the tenancy of an apartment in Hampton Court Palace. He was refused.
Possibly his comment about Lord North worked against him. Locally, the
old Prime Minister was seen as a harmless and benign figure. As Ranger, his
widow, Lady North, stayed on at Bushy House until her death in 1797
allowed the opportunity of a royal successor.

The next Ranger of Bushy Park was William, Duke of Clarence, third
son of George III. When he became Ranger he was a minor royal, a failed
sea captain, chronically in debt and of somewhat doubtful reputation. He
had long held ambitions as a gentleman farmer, which may be why he
was given Bushy Park. It is more likely that the royal advisers were
becoming increasingly alarmed at the the public nature of his disrep-
utable life-style and thought to place him in a rural position away from
the spotlight of London life.

For some years he had been living openly with the greatest comedy
actress of the day, known as Dorothy, or Dora, Jordan. They already had
three children, and another seven were to be born to them at Bushy House.

Almost the first act of William when he became Ranger was to have the
last of the Tudor timber oaks and other trees felled, and 758 trees were
sold for a handsome profit. He continued to turn trees into a cash crop
and a year after he arrived the park was almost denuded of trees. He also
enclosed over half the park to make new arable and pasture; in effect,
most of Bushy Park became his private farm.

Fig. 24 *William, Duke
of Clarence*

Fig. 25 *Dorothy Jordan as Rosalind
in 'As you like it'*

A complex of barns and farm buildings including a farm bailiff's cottage were built near the Canal Plantation (see MAP VI page 38). Nearby there was an existing house which was later granted as a Grace and Favour residence to the son of Sir John Barton, financial adviser to the Duke of Clarence. William Barton himself was both Secretary and Librarian to the Duke. When Queen Adelaide became Ranger on William's accession, Barton acted as Deputy Ranger of Bushy Park. The farm buildings were demolished in 1851, although the house is there still as a Grace and Favour residence and known as Barton's Cottage.

William was always short of money; Dora Jordan helped to keep him and to pay for the upkeep of Bushy House out of her own earnings on the stage. She and William were devoted parents to their children and made alterations to the top floor of the house to accommodate their extensive family and the assorted nursery maids and servants needed to care for them. The architect, John Nash was busy planning these alterations which included the addition of a colonnaded porch to the west front.

Later, Nash was to undertake the conversion of apartments in St James's Palace into Clarence House for William. When he became King, he chose to use Clarence House as his London home rather than Buckingham Palace of which he said, 'Hideous: turn it into a barracks.'

One of William's most valued friends from the days of his naval career was Lord Nelson. William was a guest at his friend's marriage and gave away the bride. The Admiral's death at the Battle of Trafalgar grieved him deeply. A part of the foremast of the *Victory* against which Lord Nelson was standing when he received his fatal wound was placed in a small temple in the garden at Bushy House where robins nested in the shot hole to the delight of William.

When William became King and moved to Windsor Castle the mast, which weighed over half a ton, went with him. There it stayed until Edward VII gave it to the Royal United Services Club Museum. When the museum was broken up, it disappeared from view.

In 1995, the Museum Curator of the National Physical Laboratory, Sue Osborne, set out to trace the mast with a view to returning it to Bushy House. The trail led to the repository of the National Portrait Gallery where it had been stored for many decades. By then, the Curator of *Victory* had heard of the search and was jubilant at the prospect of adding it to the Nelson collection. And so the mast was dispatched to Portsmouth and William's memento of his friend was destined never to return to Bushy House.

William joined in the life of the community with great spirit. He entertained with generous hospitality and attended cricket matches, races and boxing matches. He spent many a rowdy evening at the Toye Inn near

Hampton Court Bridge, drinking and playing cards with his neighbours in Hampton and doubtless catching up with the local gossip. Now demolished, the Toye was an ancient hostelry which had been much visited by Cromwell's soldiers.

The threat of war with the French was still present. In 1803, the inhabitants of Teddington turned out as 'Volunteers of Infantry and Cavalry' in case their services were required. The Duke of Clarence joined the meeting and entered his name in the ranks. He promised that 'not only would he go with them wherever they were needed but would stay by them till they returned to their homes'. The report in *The Times* newspaper was fulsome in its praise, 'We know not how to express our admiration of the conduct of his Royal Highness on this occasion.'

There were many famous birthday celebrations for William at Bushy House when his brothers joined in the fun of music and feasting. The local inhabitants were allowed to enjoy the occasions vicariously by looking through the windows at the splendours of the royal banquet. Toast after toast was drunk accompanied by cannon fire. Military bands played and dancing on the moonlit lawns continued to the small hours. On one famous occasion, the Prince of Wales sang a duet with Mrs Jordan. This occasion was the subject of a scathing attack by the radical journalist William Cobbett in the *Political Register*.

By 1811, though, the happy family life in Bushy Park was breaking up. Dora's earning power was diminishing in her middle years and William still needed money. His brother was made Prince Regent as the illness of their father progressed and it gradually became apparent that this ignored and disliked third son of George III might indeed be in line to inherit the throne one day.

William began looking for a suitable bride and had proposed marriage to at least one heiress; after twenty years Dora Jordan had to go. She left Bushy House abruptly.

William gave the responsibility of providing for Dora to his financial adviser, Sir John Barton. He, though, was more interested in keeping up the Duke's income than supporting William's ex-mistress. Dora eventually fled to France in

Fig. 27 *The reason so many local pubs are named after Clarence and his widow is that in the first year of his reign an act was passed allowing anybody to open an alehouse in his own home on payment of a licence fee of £3 a year. The idea was to steer the lower classes away from foreign drinks such as tea, coffee and especially chocolate which for over four hundred years had been regarded as an aphrodisiac. The new alehouse keepers showed their gratitude by naming their inns after the local royalty*

DUKE of CLARENCE

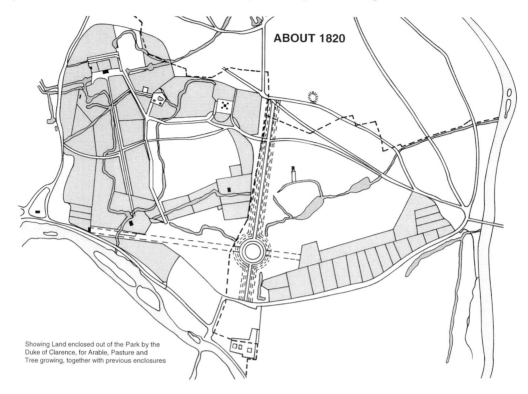

Showing Land enclosed out of the Park by the
Duke of Clarence, for Arable, Pasture and
Tree growing, together with previous enclosures

MAP VI

1815 to escape her creditors and died in poverty just under a year later at Saint-Cloud, near Paris.

By normal standards, William's conduct is indefensible. One charitable view is that he may not even have known what was happening to Dora. He had discarded her, handed on the responsiblity for her maintenance to a trusted official and had other interests to occupy him.

In 1817 the only legitimate child of the Prince Regent, Princess Charlotte, died in childbirth and the Prince Regent himself was in poor health. That left the Duke of York in line to inherit the crown and, after him, William. A frantic tour to search out a princess who was prepared to marry him took William to Europe and in 1818, Princess Adelaide of Saxe-Meiningen, became his bride.

William brought his new wife back to Bushy House in the spring of the following year. The Duchess, who spoke little English, arrived in a strange country to a houseful of children by her husband's ex-mistress. She was a gentle person and was

Fig. 26 *Queen Adelaide*

affectionate and motherly to her ready-made family in spite of the deaths in infancy of her own two little daughters. On the occasion of his marriage, William was granted a proper allowance to meet his new status as a married duke and was no longer in such severe financial straits.

Bushy House was enlarged during his occupation. A set of accurate plans was drawn up by Sir John Soane in 1797, the year William moved to Bushy. Only minor repairs were performed on the house until William's marriage, but in 1820 £4000 was spent in adding extra rooms and offices. By 1832 the house was more or less as it is now. By that time, the Duke of York had died and William was already King.

On William's accession to the throne, the local community arranged a 'grand public entertainment' in honour of their most famous resident. The poor of the district were given a great feast; rustic sports and fireworks took place. Two illuminated triumphal arches, complete with flags and flowers, were erected across the Hampton Court Road: one close to the park gates at Clarence Place which was the home of the builder to the Duke of Clarence, and the other at the Toye Inn by Hampton Court Bridge. An address was presented by local dignitaries to the new King and Queen expressing their loyalty.

In his reply to this testimony the King announced that as a mark of his affection for the neighbourhood, he had appointed Queen Adelaide as Ranger in his stead. William then endeared himself still further to his loyal subjects by giving express orders for the 'free admission of the public to Bushy Palace [*sic*] and to the Park'.

After William died in 1837 Queen Adelaide continued to use Bushy House as one of her official residences. The conservatory, or vine house, in the gardens near the house dates from the early years of her occupation. It was designed by Sir Jeffry Wyatville who was also advising the Dowager Queen's brother, the Duke of Saxe-Meiningen, on his plans for a castle in Landsberg, Germany. It was Wyatville who was responsible for the massive restoration works at Windsor Castle which were destroyed in the fire of 1992.

Adelaide occupied herself with her library and her needlework which she contributed to charitable bazaars throughout the kingdom. She gave generously to local causes including schools and churches, and eight hundred poor families in Hampton Court, Hampton, Hampton Hill and Teddington received yearly gifts of beef and bread at Christmas from the Dowager Queen. She was held in great affection and at her death in 1849 was much mourned. Only after her death did it become apparent that nearly half her income had been given to charity, although, strangely, no provision had been made for pensions for her staff, not even for those 'grown grey in her service'.

One long-serving member of staff, although not grown grey at the time of Queen Adelaide's death, was Thomas Foster. His father had been employed as an under-keeper to the Duke of Clarence and Thomas was brought up in a keeper's cottage in Bushy Park. From an early age, Thomas earned a few pence by minding cattle and opening the gates for the Duke when he was out riding.

Fig. 29 *Thomas Foster*

When Queen Adelaide died, Thomas had been working as an under-gardener at Bushy House for many years. The gardens were renowned and covered over 30 acres. There were roses and honeysuckle in the pleasure gardens, grapes and geraniums under glass, while the kitchen gardens produced vegetables of fine quality. However, Thomas had to wait until the next century for a pension. He continued to work as a gardener in the village of Hampton until he was eighty-six.

In 1909, Thomas was the oldest inhabitant of Hampton Hill and, at the age of ninety, among the first to receive the Old Age Pension. According to the *Surrey Comet* of January that year, 'no man could be more deserving, he having maintained himself for the past four years out of his hard-earned savings which are now nearly exhausted'.

Bushy House was cared for by only a skeleton staff until, in 1865, it was offered by Queen Victoria to the Duc de Nemours, second son of Louis-Philippe, Duc d'Orleans, the exiled King of France.

Previously, when the new country of Belgium was formed in 1831, Louis-Philippe was struggling to strengthen the foreign influence of France. He made strenuous efforts to acquire the newly-established throne for his second son. His machinations were doomed to failure. This proposal was vetoed by other countries, including Britain. Instead, the throne went to Leopold of Saxe-Coburg. Later, with a change of political climate, the Duc went to England.

The biographer of the Duc de Nemours paints a dismal picture of his time at Bushy Park.

> It is impossible to visit Bushy House in the season without thinking of the sadness which must fall with the rain, with the mist, with the wind on this flat deserted landscape.

This impression contrasts with the eloquent praise of an account published in the previous decade in *The Beauties of Middlesex* by William Keane which describes the gardens as,

> . . . exquisitely lovely pleasure grounds, . . . composed of various scenes; from some points are fine open views of the park, the free flowing undulations of the green velvet lawn are diversified by groups, clumps and single trees, and the broad walks are carried through the ever-changing open vistas or bowery groups of the home grounds . . .

Even after Nemours was allowed to return to France, he kept Bushy House on as a possible refuge in case of future trouble and used it as a storehouse for his considerable possessions. Interestingly, after much correspondence about the subject, he was forced to pay local rates while living in Bushy House.

After the Duc's death in 1896, his son returned Bushy House to the Crown. Queen Victoria had no use for it and proposed an exchange for two houses in Pall Mall held by the Commissioners of Woods and Forests to use as Grace and Favour apartments. The Crown, though, insisted on approving the use to which Bushy House would be put.

Fig. 28 *Vine House designed by Sir Jeffery Wyatville for Queen Adelaide*

There was a good solution available. The Royal Society had been trying to find a home for its proposed National Standards Laboratory for some time. Finally, after other sites had been found unsuitable, Bushy House was suggested. After some negotiation this was approved and the National Physical Laboratory was created under its first director, Richard Glazebrook. The upper part of the house became the residence of the Director and the ground floor and basement were used as laboratories. Other buildings were added as needed, usually in a red-brick style that more or less harmonised with the original. More land was added to the original estate by purchase, reaching as far as the Hampton Road.

The National Physical Laboratory, known world-wide as the NPL, has been a centre of excellence since its inception. It carries out research and provides services of great importance to industry, government departments and many other organisations. The scientific work of the laboratory covers most areas of physics, information technology and computing. Its fundamental research at the frontiers of science together with its National Measurements System affect all aspects of everyday life. Experiments carried out in its wind tunnels directly influenced the development of the Spitfire aircraft in the Second World War. The earliest experiments in radar were carried out on NPL's sports field and when war came in 1939, this meant Britain was already in the forefront of radar technology. Barnes Wallis carried out essential tests for the development of his bouncing bombs in the NPL ship tanks and one of the world's earliest electronic computers (now in the Science Museum in Kensington), was built by NPL scientists.

Today, the research carried out at NPL leads the international scientific field in many areas and Bushy House still contains working laboratories. Top scientific work is carried out in rooms previously occupied by the kitchens and domestic quarters more used to the clatter and bustle of the household servants of past years who had served the successive colourful Rangers of Bushy Park.

Fig. 30 *View of the Queen's Lodge, Bushy Park (with dedication to Queen Adelaide) by H B Ziegler c. 1830*

Fig. 31 *Garden temple at Bushy House. A portion of the mast from the 'Victory' was placed here by the Duke of Clarence*

Fig. 32 *The Longford River in autumn*

Fig. 33 *View of Longford River outside the west wall of Bushy Park with Hampton smock mill (demolished 1870s.) c. 1860, unattributed. The figure in the foreground is carrying buckets with water. It was illegal to take water from the Longford River although this was ignored by local people. At that time, it was the only source of running water*

4. THE LONGFORD RIVER

Although Hampton Court Palace was by the Thames, it was always short of water. There was a pressurised supply of drinking water from a conduit head at Coombe Hill, although the water was not used for cooking vegetables as it was reputed to turn them black. This was either caused by the lead pipe which carried it across the bed of the Thames or from some other contamination. Whatever the cause, the water was much praised for its sweetness. There was another wooden pipe from the enclosure called Spring Grove at Hampton; and a reservoir in the North Park (see MAP III) which was fed by several local springs and supplied the palace fountains. Nevertheless, the ponds in the gardens had originally been filled at night by labourers who pumped the water up from wells using a treadmill. There was nowhere locally with a sufficient fall of water to run a millwheel. The local springs were none too reliable and in years of low rainfall they could dry up almost completely.

In the later 1630s, Charles I, or his advisers, had the idea of constructing an artificial canal from the Colne River to provide an extra and reliable supply of water to the gardens. There was a  precedent; the Duke of Northumberland's River had been cut from the Colne River to feed the Brazil Mills at Isleworth about a century earlier. ('Brazil' was a red dyestuff made from the wood of a tropical hardwood tree. Chaucer referred to it in his *Canterbury Tales*. The South American country is named after the dye, not the other way round.) A commission was set up in 1638 under the Chancellor of the Exchequer, Lord Cottington, to arrange the details of the project.

Fig. 34 *Charles I*

A contractor, Edward Manning, was put in charge of the construction of the canal. He already had experience in a similar field: when Richmond Park was being enclosed about 1635, Manning had been paid for 'walling, ponds, and cutting lawns in the new park at Richmond, and bringing a river through the same'. On 22 October 1638 a warrant was issued to pay him £3000 'for cutting a new river from Longford to His Ma'ties house at Hampton Court'. A further payment was made in January 1640 for 'perfecting of divers things about the New River from Longford'. The project was completed in a mere nine months and eight days.

The Longford River was almost as unpopular as Richmond New Park had been. It cut through the middle of Hounslow Heath, blocking roads and dividing the lands of the parishes it crossed. To make things worse it was poorly-made, leaky and too shallow to cope with flood conditions on the Colne. There was occasional flooding of pasture and even arable land along its whole length.

The labourers charged with maintaining the river were not paid during 1642 or 1643, although Manning still had £700 left of the money allowed to the project. The Civil War was a good excuse for him, but an even better chance for the locals who so detested the river.

In 1649 about a hundred of the inhabitants of the parishes on Hounslow Heath went to Longford, broke down the bridge there, and dammed the river with stones and gravel.

For years the Longford River did not run. In 1653, Hampton parishioners, probably prompted by Parliament who wanted to sell the parks, petitioned to reopen it. There was disagreement from the people of Hanworth and Feltham; they pleaded that they should not be ruined 'for the private ends of some few'. The dignitaries of Kingston pointed out that the river was 'a very great nuisance' and that it blocked the roads. The enquiry produced no result at all; the river stayed empty. When Cromwell had fish-ponds dug in the Harewarren for his sport they were fed not from the Longford River but from local springs within the park. In 1659, after his death, the river was still dry.

After the Restoration, Charles II decided that Hampton Court needed the water from Longford to supply the new Long Water in the House (or Home) Park to Hampton Court Palace, which he was having re-organised into a small copy of the park at Versailles. Adrian May, a Groom of the

Fig. 35 *Charles II. Unblocking the Longford River caused mixed reactions*

Privy Chamber and supervisor of the gardens at Hampton Court, was given the task of 'bringing the water to Hampton Courte, for planting there, . . . and for other His Ma'ties secrett services . . .' The King's most trusted courtiers were sometimes charged with carrying out sensitive dealings for him away from the public gaze and these assignments were referred to in the record books simply as 'secret service'.

Edward Manning felt aggrieved that he had been passed over for the task. He petitioned that he had 'lost £10,000 in the late King's cause, a Parliamentary Captain torturing his servant to discover his money and plate . . . and had cut the New River from Colebrook to Hampton Court'. Eventually, he was allowed the job of replacing and maintaining the bridges over the Longford River, a duty which he neglected in much the same way as he had failed to ensure proper standards in cutting the Longford River itself. Complaints about their bad state of repair appeared regularly.

When the Longford water was restored to Hampton Court a few new problems appeared. The original route of the river led past Upper Lodge to the reservoir, now in the Waterhouse Woodland Gardens, which was a head for the palace fountains. Over a large part of its course it had to be built up to run well above ground level because the land fell away so swiftly. When constructing the Longford, Manning had routed it along some of the medieval field edges which still stand higher than the land around them, so that he could save money and effort in constructing the banks. From the old reservoir the river was taken to the gate near the palace and under the road to feed the ponds in the garden to the east which is now known as Fountain Garden. It then discharged eastward to a natural stream entering the Thames near Kingston Bridge.

Adrian May, as well as making the Long Water in the House Park, decided to add another branch in Bushy Park to augment the springs that supplied Cromwell's fish-ponds in the Harewarren. The result was that the ponds regularly overfilled, flooding the ancient highway through the Harewarren from Hampton Wick to Teddington Common. It is possible still to see how the banks of the Leg of Mutton Pond, then called 'Oliver's Pond', have been built up to contain the flooding.

After some time and much work, the river settled down into a more or less stable state. The man who was mainly responsible for its eventual orderliness was Thomas Simpson. Appointed when Edward Proger was Ranger, he was a keeper in Bushy Park for almost seventy years and for at least fifty of those he was either performing work on the Longford River or completely in charge of the cleaning and maintenance of the section of it inside the parks.

Simpson was probably the first occupant of the White Lodge at the western end of the lime avenue leading from the Diana Pond, though it is unlikely that he ever used it as his main residence; he already owned several houses by the time the White Lodge was built. After he died the lodge referred to as 'late Simpson's' was in so ruinous a condition that it was considered cheaper to rebuild it than repair it.

Thomas Simpson was no mere shovel wielder; in his will he described himself as a 'gentleman', a status higher than a yeoman but lower than the rank of armiger who was a man entitled to bear heraldic arms. He organised and sub-contracted the work rather than doing it himself. When he fell ill in 1726, the Earl of Halifax (George Montagu) wanted to appoint one of his own men in Simpson's place if he should die. He did not, in fact, die for another eight years, on 13 September 1734, still in harness at the age of ninety-nine. His wife Ann had died two years earlier aged a hundred and six. They were buried in Hampton parish church.

In about 1710 the Longford River was diverted into a new high pond at Upper Lodge as part of the Earl of Halifax's water gardens. Two years later when it was decided to transfer the statue in the Privy Gardens at Hampton Court, now known as 'Diana', to the new pond in Chestnut

Avenue as centrepiece, the extra head of water provided by the Upper Lodge pond made it possible to make the plinth on which the statue stood much higher. The rather feeble flow of the original fountain was considerably improved, and new bronze castings were made by Richard Osgood and others to embellish the plinth and 'spout the water'.

The making of the Diana Pond was the last major change in the Longford River as far as Bushy Park was concerned. Other incidents happened outside the park. In the early eighteenth century there were complaints that some of the people through whose land the river flowed were cutting the banks and stealing the water.

Fig. 36 *Diana Fountain*

The paper mills at Longford were bought by the Crown in 1717 to ensure that the water supply to the river was not impeded by the owner of the mills.

By 1850 the pipe from Upper Lodge to the Diana Fountain was no longer supplying water and the fountain had stopped running. After the pipe from Coombe Hill Conduit House to Hampton Court Palace was fractured by a steamship in 1876, filter beds were set up by the water mill at Hanworth and Longford water was pumped to a cistern in the palace for drinking. Licences were still in existence at the turn of the century for the water to be drawn off for drinking at the public houses near the Hampton Court Gate. At the same time a new pipe was laid from the catchpit at the water mill to supply the Diana Fountain and the fountains at the palace under gravity.

The Longford River is no longer the nuisance it once was. It does not flood or dry up, nor is it now regarded as a major obstacle to travellers. Its meandering course is edged with willows, sedge and rushes; perch, roach and tench glide through the water, dragonflies dance on the surface, water voles hide in its banks and the Longford River is now one of the delights of Bushy Park.

5. CHESTNUT AVENUE

The most celebrated feature of Bushy Park is the long tree-lined road leading through the park from Teddington to Hampton Court. Four rows of lime trees on each side have been interlined with horse chestnuts whose pink-and-white candle-like blossoms in May have been acclaimed so widely.

The original reason for the making of Chestnut Avenue has disappeared; indeed, had gone before it was finished. In the late seventeenth century, Sir Christopher Wren, Surveyor to the King, was rebuilding Hampton Court Palace. To his eye, the Tudor buildings there were old-fashioned and unsightly. Wren had plans to completely redesign the palace to contemporary standards. His proposals included a grand new approach from the north which would cross the road and finish in a colonnaded courtyard. During this construction, most of the remains of the Tudor palace would have been destroyed. Chestnut Avenue was to be that grand approach. William III died before the scheme could be completely carried out and luckily it is still possible to see the Tudor remnants of the palace.

Fig. 37 *Sir Christopher Wren*

Wren designed the Great Avenue but its development was supervised by William Talman, Comptroller of the King's Works. The actual planting and road building was initially started by George London, although the project was taken over by Henry Wise. George London had travelled to France where he had admired the wide use there of horse chestnut trees. On his return he decided to add these to the original scheme of a lime-edged avenue.

Work started in the summer of 1699. The Great Avenue was not aligned with any feature in Bushy Park; it was intended to feed across the Hampton Court Road straight into the centre of Wren's colonnaded entrance court. So the Tudor wall that separated the Middle Park from the Harewarren had to be demolished because its northern part crossed the projected line of the new avenue. The old gates to the park at Teddington and Hampton Court were left in position for a while, but new gates and gate lodges at the ends of the new avenue were added.

The trees that Wise planted were not mere saplings but mature specimens, three or four feet in girth, taken from established stands. Wren's Great Avenue was intended to be an impressive piece of work from the start, already magnificent even before his new palace was finished to act as its focus.

More or less by accident, since both ends were already fixed before it was laid out, the length of the avenue is almost exactly a mile. The distance between the lines of chestnuts is 170 feet (52 metres) and the road through them was originally 60 feet wide (18 metres). It was metalled with gravel dug from pits just outside the western edge of the trees. The pits later had their edges sloped so they were no longer dangerous to riders, and some of them can still be seen.

At the point where the Longford River crossed the new road, a large circular pond was constructed, four hundred feet (120 metres) across and five feet (1.5 metres) deep. From the pond, two extra avenues of limes were planted at right angles to the Great Avenue. The eastern one was never finished, though it was probably intended to reach as far as Hampton Wick. In fact, it ended at the fence at the end of the Paddock Course where there was a sanctuary for deer which outran pursuing hounds.

The western avenue had as its focus a new keeper's lodge, now called White Lodge. The earth dug from the pond, some 20,000 tons, was used to fill low spots along the side avenues.

The road was taken around the pond on both sides and the tree line carried outside the road in a circle. But after the road left the south side of the pond, Wren meant to set the trees back away from the road, so as to open up the view of his new palace. That scheme was never carried out.

The Great Avenue planting was finished by the end of 1699. It had cost only £3000 plus another £1050 for digging the pond. Of that only £219 had been spent on actually transplanting the 274 chestnuts and 1000 limes. By far the greatest expense, £3025, had been making the road itself, with over 30,000 tons of fine screened gravel.

A glorious confusion surrounds the origin of the fountain and statue

Fig. 38 *Queen Henrietta Maria. Charles I commissioned two fountains for her garden at Somerset House, London*

which were later placed in the basin in Chestnut Avenue. The statue has been named (often at the same time) as Arethusa, Diana and even Venus. Part of the confusion springs from the abundance of statuary available in the seventeenth century. Not only were sculptors commissioned for specific pieces, but also agents scoured Italy for statuary to add to the collections of both the Crown and wealthy buyers in England. Certainly, Charles I used such agents. Almost always of mythical figures, the statues were often moved around between royal residences. If there was no place for them at a particular time, they were put into boxes and stored.

Charles I was a great patron of painters and sculptors. His importance as a collector and connoisseur is now widely recognised. Charles commissioned the

French sculptor, Hubert Le Sueur, to provide two fountains for the garden of his Queen, Henrietta Maria, at the royal residence of Somerset House in London. Inigo Jones was Surveyor to the Crown at the time. A record in 1637 of a payment to Le Sueur reads 'for brasse and marble work done by him for a Fountayne in Her Mats. Garden at Somerset House according with severall Bargaines made with him by Inigoe Jones, Esq. Surveyor of her Mats. workes'.

About four years earlier, Inigo Jones had sketched a preliminary study for a fountain (see Fig 39). Although a fully worked-out scheme has not been discovered, several elements of this drawing such as the fish-holding *putti,* the shells and the mermaids, were included by Le Sueur in this fountain and show the influence of Inigo Jones on the completed design.

Whether the statue was initially designed as a Diana is uncertain. Certainly, accounts in 1637 record Le Sueur's fee of £200 for a 'great Diana' although it is not clear to which of his statues this referred. The statue has none of the identifying

Fig. 39 *Sketch by Inigo Jones*

attributes of the goddess Diana, such as the crescent moon on her head or her bow or hunting dog, although her pose and dress are those traditionally associated with a Diana.

Fig. 40 *Photograph of the statue of 'Diana' taken during restoration*

An inventory made in 1651 refers to one of these fountains in meticulous detail. This description matches the fountain now in Bushy Park although the subject of the great statue surmounting it is not named.

In 1656, while Oliver Cromwell was Lord Protector, the fountain and statue were removed to the gardens of Hampton Court Palace and in about 1690, the fountain was set up in the Privy Garden with the statue on a new scrolled stone pedestal made by Edward Pierce.

After the Restoration, the diarist, John Evelyn, made a passing reference in 1662 to the fountain as being by the Italian sculptor, Francesco Fanelli, and this has been taken ever since as unquestioned fact.

It was not until restoration work in 1976 that the bronzes could be closely examined and photographed and then questions began to be asked about their tenuous connection with Fanelli. Dr Charles Avery, at that time Deputy Keeper of the Sculpture Department at the Victoria and Albert Museum, studied the bronzes at first hand and ordered new photographs for a comparison of details. He demonstrated convincingly that the style is consistent with that of Le Sueur, as manifested on the great tombs in Westminster Abbey and elsewhere, whereas Fanelli's work is far more lively in movement and modelling (see: *Hubert Le Sueur, 'the Unworthy Praxiteles of King Charles I'* The Walpole Society, XLVIII, 1982, pp. 135 – 209).

The drawing by Inigo Jones for the fountain was first published by Geoffrey Fisher and John Newman (see: *A fountain design by Inigo Jones* The Burlington Magazine, vol. CXXVII, 1985, pp. 531–532).

During an inventory of 1659, the statue was referred to as Arethusa, possibly because that nymph had been turned into a fountain as a disguise against a pursuing river god.

After much regilding, recasting and the carving of an additional base, the statue and fountain were moved to Bushy Park in 1713 to take up residence in the huge basin in Chestnut Avenue. No trace of the gilding remains today. Written records of this expensive work refer to the statue as 'Diana'. A hundred years ago, however, the proper designation was still causing puzzlement locally. The *Surrey Comet* of 20 October 1897 summed up the current bewilderment in the following verse:

> Oh goddess, prithee tell me true
> Which of the goddesses are you?
> Must we confess that, to our shame
> We've called you your half-sister's name
> And in a most unclassic manner
> Have dubbed our Venus, a Diana?

Today the statue, collectively with the basin and fountain, is known and loved by all as 'The Diana'.

From the start, the Great Avenue was a private royal road, not to be used without authorisation. It was to be a further link in the route for the King's coach which ran from St James's Palace, through Sloane Square and the King's Road and then to Hampton Court. A rail was put down each side of it to separate it from the rest of the park. The ancient highway for pedestrians and vehicles from Hampton Wick to Teddington Heathgate through the Harewarren, which well antedated any of the parks, was closed and a new road, Sandy Lane, made outside the park fence in its stead. For a while, this became the responsibility of the Surveyor of the King's Roads, along with the Great Avenue itself.

ig. 41 *Lion Gates c. 1820-22 by Thomas Rowlandson*

The Chestnuts in Bushey Park.

Fig. 42 *Etching of Chestnut Avenue in flower with Diana Fountain and deer*

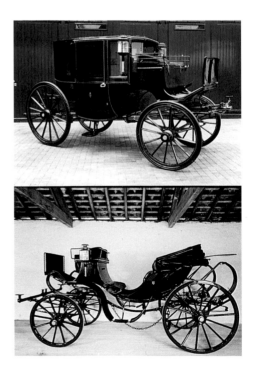

Fig. 43 *Carriages: a Clarence (above) and a Victoria (below). Both royal namesakes drove along Chestnut Avenue*

Another way across Bushy Park from Hampton Town's End to Hampton Wick was closed at the same time. The Hampton villagers had been in the habit of strolling through the park on their way to Kingston Market probably crossing the former wall between the Middle Park and the Harewarren by a ladderstile. But there was no way for them to do so now without crossing the Great Avenue, which was, of course, forbidden. A young shoemaker named Timothy Bennett missed seeing them pass his shop in Hampton Wick High Street. Over fifty years later he engaged in a popular campaign to re-open that footpath, which is now miscalled 'Cobbler's Walk'. Timothy was a shoemaker, a cordwainer, and would definitely have felt insulted to have been represented as a cobbler, a mere shoe repairer. However, as a name, 'Cordwainer's Walk' does not have the same ring somehow.

Fig. 44 *Timothy Bennett*

William III's death in November 1702 meant the end of work on Wren's new Palace. Queen Anne had no interest in it and cancelled the project. The Great Avenue was retained, however, and remained a royal road, even though the original reason for its making no longer existed. The locals were allowed into Bushy Park but they still could not cross the Great Avenue on their way to the Wick.

In 1710 a set of grassy roads was laid out in both Bushy Park and Home Park for Queen Anne to be led around in her chaise, to give her amusement and exercise. She was past driving herself and already in poor health.

The chaise ridings were planned by Henry Wise and the work involved levelling molehills, digging ditches and watercourses and removing nettles and weeds thereby 'putting into Order Chaise Ridings fitt for Her Maj'tey's Ease and Safety'. The work cost £806 and in Bushy Park the ridings covered over twenty miles.

One of Queen Anne's chaise ridings followed the eastern course of the footpath formerly used by the Hampton villagers to go to Hampton Wick; another two ran each side of the Great Avenue between the lime trees. There had been two turnpike gates in the rails alongside the Great Avenue to allow carriages to leave it, probably leading to the lodges in the Middle Park and the Harewarren. Others must have been added for the chaise ridings to cross the avenue.

The Great Avenue continued to be maintained by the King's Surveyor as a private royal road for decades. In the late 1740s, though, a campaign was building among the gentry to re-open the roads through Richmond Park which had originally been stopped up to protect game. At first the objectors were not successful, but in the summer of 1752 their efforts were given a boost by the widespread publication of a leaflet with an engraving of the Hampton Wick shoemaker Timothy Bennett, by then seventy-five years old.

According to the engraving Timothy Bennett had caused the old path across Bushy Park to be re-opened by a 'Vigorous Application of the Laws of his Country in the Cause of Liberty'. Whether he was sparked off in his effort by the Richmond Park campaign or whether he was actually co-opted by the campaigners as a figure-head to provide an example which they could use against the Ranger of Richmond Park is unclear. What is certain is the enthusiasm the Richmond campaigners showed to him. They must have provided the finance for the making and distribution of the engraving and the publicity campaign which accompanied it. It does not seem to have been too difficult to get the footpath re-opened; Bennett did not actually have to go to law. He may even have been acting in collusion with the second Earl of Halifax, the Ranger of Bushy Park at the time. The stiles at the ends of the footpath (see MAP V) seem never to have been closed. They were still there when the present wall round Bushy Park was built in 1734–7. However events were contrived, it would seem that Bennett's success was welcomed by the Richmond Park campaigners.

The story has grown considerably over the years as all legends must. Halifax gained his present reputation as an arrogant ursurper of the people's privileges long after everybody who knew the facts was dead. After all, for a decent story one has to have a villain as well as a hero. But it was certainly not Halifax who had the idea of closing the path. At that time, he had not been born.

After 1752 there is no further mention of the Great Avenue as a royal road. The footpath across it became official instead of merely traditional. A narrow gravel path can be detected running just north of the present Cobbler's Walk, to pass outside the bracken instead of through it as the modern one does. This was almost certainly the original route.

When the footpath was re-opened again, people started to linger and wander off the path as they walked through the park. From then on it would seem that no attempts were made to stop access to the park and it became fashionable to ride and picnic on the grasslands, athough permission had to be sought to ride down the Great Avenue.

James Boswell, chronicler of Dr Johnson, wrote in his Journal in 1785 that he felt 'vastly well' after he had 'dined in Bushy Park in the air'. The composition of the picnic is not described.

The state of the country's road system improved with proper maintenance from the turnpike trusts. In 1767 coach traffic increased with the establishment of local trusts. Daily coaches ran from London to Hampton Court along the Great Avenue. The King's Arms Inn and the Toye at Hampton Court were both staging posts for changing horses.

The Great Avenue came to be called the Chestnut Avenue at some time during the nineteenth century and the original road was raised as a causeway and halved in width. Perhaps the Duke of Clarence in his perpetual search for money had sold the gravel, as he sold some of the lime trees of the Avenue.

In Victorian times, after the palace was opened to the public, Chestnut Avenue became a popular place of resort for Londoners. A trip to Bushy Park at any time was a day of high excitement for families who would arrive in various horse-drawn vehicles from the squalor of the East End of London on summer Sundays. There are accounts that the noise of singing, fiddles and accordions overpowered the hymn-singing of the worshippers at Kingston parish church.

Fig. 45 *Picnic under the Trees, 1851*

A report in *The Times* of August 12, 1835 states that 'Not less than 25 van loads of mechanics, with their wives and children, have arrived in one day at Hampton Court to enjoy a picnic repast in Bushy Park.'

Fig. 46 *A day out for the school children, 1849*

The Ragged Schools were first begun early in the nineteenth century to give free education to the poorest children and were later formed into an official union under Lord Shaftesbury. A yearly treat for some of these children was a day's outing to Bushy Park and disabled children from the Home Cripples Branch were also included. Drinking water fountains were erected especially to meet their needs. Children, then as now, revelled in the freedom they found in the park.

The habit grew of visiting the Great Avenue in the late spring during the weeks when the chestnuts were in full bloom. Eventually this was regularised with the help of the newspapers who publicised it into a yearly event, called Chestnut Sunday. Indeed, a journalist on the *Richmond and Twickenham Times*, Jim Blewett, claimed to have invented Chestnut Sunday about 1890. He would

Fig. 47 *Chestnut Sunday, 1881*

Fig. 48 *The last bus back to London, 1847*

watch the chestnuts and inform the London newspapers when they were about to come into flower. The local publicans would also club together to advertise the flowering. The Londoners would then turn up on the next Sunday in their thousands to admire the candle-like blossoms.

Chestnut Sunday lost some of its popularity after the First World War and was virtually abandoned after the Second. It has now come back into fashion, but as a far more organised and less boisterous affair than it used to be. The hare coursing, donkey races and swearing matches so popular with day-trippers of the previous century are events of the past.

Also popular with the hard-working people from London was the grand military event of 1871 when Queen Victoria reviewed her troops in Bushy Park. The Household Troops and Artillery were commanded by a nephew of Queen Adelaide, Prince Edward of Saxe Weimar. Prince Edward was born at Bushy House and remained in England to become a regular officer of the British Army.

Fig. 49 *Queen Victoria's Review of the Troops*

So great was the press of carriages containing members of the royal family that many thousands of spectators remained outside the park where they were perfectly content to hurl their own comments at the carriage trade and to take part in far more interesting pastimes. Vendors had set up stalls selling pickled whelks and pigs' trotters. Fiddlers played the latest dance tunes. There were favourite games to join in, with one called 'Kiss in the Ring' attracting the most interest. There was a fire eater and there were jugglers and the local inns did a roaring trade. Altogether, a grand day out for everyone.

Later in her reign, Queen Victoria became embroiled in a heated dispute over firewood in the park. There had long been an ancient right of 'lop and top' where people collected discarded wood in the park.

A wrangle developed between different government departments as to whether the poor should be allowed to gather fallen branches or whether it was the perquisite of a government official.

The Queen vigorously defended the rights of the Crown to allow the poor to take the wood and actually called on Mr Gladstone, her prime minister, to vindicate the position. Finally, she suggested that to avoid any possibility of trouble in the future, she should be appointed Ranger of the Park herself. Horrified, Mr Gladstone quickly pointed out that the position of Ranger carried a salary of £600 a year and income earned in such a way was incompatible with the Crown and its wearer.

Fig. 50 *Cycle Meet. Large crowds gathered to admire the riders*

The dispute faded with time and, as reported in the newspaper article which recalled the incident, 'The poor get their wood if not by right, as a privilege and it would now be hard to take away even if it were desired to do so.'

The penny-farthing bicycle was an invention which was ridden only by the young, fit and fearless. The penny-farthing or 'Ordinary' was inherently unstable and dangerous. Riders had to be measured for the correct size of the huge front wheel by the length of their legs. Bushy Park was the scene for the great cycle meets of the time.

The meets started in a small way in 1874 with only a few cyclists and escalated in size. In 1877, the *Scientific American* carried a report announcing to the American public: 'the largest meeting of bicycle riders that has ever been held assembled on May 25th at Hampton Court in England. The drivers extended for a mile and a quarter on the Kingston Road, and numbered between 1500 to 2000.' These 'drivers' represented their cycling clubs and were turned out smartly in club colours. The organisation of the meet was run on the lines of a military manoeuvre and orders were given by cavalry signals sounded on a bugle. A circular sent to clubs advertised training in essential skills:

Fig. 51 *Advertisement for Safety Skirt Holder. The invention of the Safety bicycle gave women the same freedom of travel as men*

> Gentlemen wishing to perfect themselves in riding are cordially invited to pay a visit to the City Bicycle School, where they can be taught to mount and dismount quickly and the art of riding slowly, etc. Novices prepared specially for the approaching meet at Hampton Court.

In a previous year the keeper of the toll-gate then existing on Hampton Court Bridge had been driven to fury when he was confronted by crowds at the end of the day, holding their bicycles over their heads and insisting that they pay the lesser toll to cross as they were foot passengers. The bridge was ceremoniously freed from tolls in 1876.

The first safety bicycle, the Rover, came into production in 1885. Ordinary men and women at last were given the opportunity of a mobility which up to then had been the privilege of those who could afford to maintain a stable of horses. Cycling now lost its exclusiveness. Two years later the *Richmond and Kingston Express* was reporting that '. . . clubs propose to parade at Hampton Court and have decided to permit (safety) bicycles to join them. We think this thing is played out.' And indeed so it was. The time of the monster cycle meets was past.

Crowds still turned out in their thousands in the early years of the twentieth century. Bushy Park was fashionable and popular with all society. Edward VII visited on several occasions and in 1910, the new King George V and his cousin, the Kaiser, drove from London through Bushy Park to Windsor to his father's state funeral in St George's Chapel. Chestnut Avenue was not at its best at that time as only two years previously a great storm had uprooted seventy lime trees and twelve chestnuts. However, new trees had been planted by the time Queen Mary made a special detour to motor through the crowds on Chestnut Avenue to admire the blossoms in 1917.

The Paddock Course running parallel to the southern boundary was now occupied by the Royal Stud. Both George IV and Queen Victoria made good profits from the yearlings bred there.

There are few of the trees which were planted by Henry Wise in Chestnut Avenue; the great storms of 1703, 1908, 1978 and 1987 laid to the ground the oldest and weakest of them. A programme of replanting the many gaps in the Avenue began in 1992 and continues under the sponsorship of the Prince of Wales Royal Parks Tree Appeal. Still admired for its stately trees, Chestnut Avenue claims a well-established affection from all who visit Bushy Park today.

6. THE TWENTIETH CENTURY

By 1850 Bushy Park looked more or less as it does today. To a large extent the park is still the creation of the Duke of Clarence. It was while he was Ranger there that most of the stands of oaks which now form such a prominent feature of the park were planted. After William became King and lost interest in farming Bushy, the large areas he had enclosed for agriculture were returned to parkland. The farm buildings he had built were demolished and the materials sold at auction in 1851. The Stockyard with its barns, stables and venison house is now used as the administrative centre for Bushy Park. A recent development has been the setting up of an Environment Centre there which is run by a team of dedicated volunteers to introduce schoolchildren to conservation in the park.

Fig. 52 *Notice of Auction of the farm buildings of the Duke of Clarence*

There was little change through the nineteenth century, even though the park was becoming more open to the public. But during the First World War some areas which had been given back to parkland were again put under the plough.

Temporary allotments were set up on the west side near Hampton and Hampton Hill and on an area adjacent to South Teddington for people to grow extra food. It is intriguing that the individual plots at Hampton were set out parallel not to the park wall there but to an old line which was once a medieval drainage ditch that ran next to the ancient road through the park from Hampton to Twickenham (see MAP III). Perhaps there was still something visible on the ground there.

After the war it was originally intended to return the allotments to parkland, but there was so much local agitation to preserve them that they were allowed to remain, except for the few near Hampton Hill. The extra land which had been ploughed, however, was given back to grass.

George V gave his permission for Upper Lodge to be turned into a convalescent home for Canadian troops. Queen Mary made a personal visit to inspect the arrangements to receive the men and she arranged for a number of games to be provided for the entertainment of the sick soldiers.

The local community also did their best to amuse the convalescents. Schools, churches and sports clubs sent out a steady stream of invitations to dance displays, football matches and musical tea parties. Seven of the most badly wounded Canadians did not survive to return home and remain buried in the parish church of St James at Hampton Hill.

During the war years, horse chestnuts were collected in response to a demand from the Ministry of Munitions who stated they were to play a vital role in the war effort. Vast quantities were gathered all over the country, mainly by schoolchildren. It was not until after the war that it was made public that the horse chestnuts had been used as a replacement for wood from which to distil acetone to manufacture cordite. Eventually only 3000 tons of chestnuts were used mainly due to difficulties of transport. For years afterwards there were piles of rotting horse chestnuts at railway stations which had been designated as collecting points.

The land which had been temporarily ploughed was returned to park, though the grass cover has still not come back to normal. It is possible to distinguish the wartime ploughland by the fact that it has different types of grass on it from the land around due to the fertiliser which had been used. The deer and other grazers prefer it and crop it closer than the rough grass in the rest of the park.

Gradually Chestnut Sunday was losing its popularity. The servant class, to whom a Sunday off was a rare treat, was rapidly declining; both men and women were finding less wearing and better paid occupations. After the reporter, Jim Blewett, retired from the *Richmond and Twickenham Times* nobody was greatly interested in telling the London papers when the chestnuts were about to come into bloom. Chestnut Sunday was abandoned for many years and has only recently been revived.

Fig. 53 *Boating pool*

We owe the 'boating pool', the triangular pool at the end of the Heron Pond, to a government scheme after the end of the First World War to provide work for the unemployed in the Royal Parks. Both before and after the Second World War it really was a boating pool; there were small rowboats and pedalos to hire and to parade solemnly around this tiny stretch of water until called in (see Fig. 53). When they were found to be uneconomic in the 1970s and removed, there were howls of disappointment not only from children but also from their parents and grandparents who had also enjoyed them. Now it is only used by model boat enthusiasts to show off their creations.

Fig. 54 *The air-breathing roots of the Swamp Cypresses in the Woodland Gardens*

Fig. 55 *Hawthorn tree in bloom*

Fig. 56 *Deer herd in Bushy Park*

In the summer of 1925, a newly created garden was opened to the public. Mr Hepburn, superintendent of the park, also used the scheme for the unemployed to good effect. The workforce he gathered had cleared undergrowth in the Waterhouse Wood and had created a woodland dell with a profusion of exotic plants and flowers such as azaleas. Cascades were made from a tributary of the Longford River and rustic bridges and winding paths completed the transformation into one of the then fashionable 'Paradise Gardens'.

From the late Forties to the late Sixties, Joseph Fisher was superintendent. His influence was equally great. He added to the charm of the Waterhouse Woodland Garden by opening up the land beneath the trees as informal lawns. He restored the eastern end, south of the Pheasantry, to the pleasure garden it had been in the 1830s. The magnificent swamp cypresses there date from that time. So successful were his changes that the local children used to call that area 'Fairyland'. He had a pond dug there which he named after his daughter Triss and, just before he retired, had yet another made which is still called 'Fishers Pond'. He even planted oaks in Bushy Park for the first time in nearly a century.

Today, the Waterhouse Garden and the Pheasantry Garden are known together as the 'Woodland Gardens' and are a riot of colour in the spring when the rhododendrons and azaleas bloom in a rainbow display.

Joseph Fisher also made changes to the way the livestock was managed. Until his time the deer were partially wintered under cover. The deer pens had mangers in them where the animals received their necessary ration of hay. Mr Fisher had the pens destroyed and the deer were allowed to live outside through the whole year, the does and hinds bearing their fawns under cover of the bracken and the winter hay pitchforked to the flock from moving lorries. He also leased grazing rights for cattle.

The Second World War saw large areas of the park go back to growing food. Again ancient lines were respected to a surprising extent. The new ploughland just north of the present Waterhouse Woodland gardens used for its eastern edge a ditch dug by John Stone in 1537 as the boundary between the park and Hampton Eastfield. The new allotments just east of Upper Lodge, now football fields, were aligned not with the Longford River, as one would expect, but with the allotments on the other side of the river, continuing the line of the old Twickenham road which was remarkable especially as the medieval ditch that showed the line of the road there had been filled in in 1687.

In the early part of the Second World War temporary buildings were put up in the park near Teddington to replace bombed-out London offices. After America entered the war in 1942 these were taken over by the United States as the nucleus of the headquarters of their Eighth Army

Air Force. It was named Camp Griffiss, after the first American officer to be killed in Europe (shot down by mistake by the RAF). Other temporary camps were made near the Laurel Road gate at Hampton Hill. The National Physical Laboratory whose work had led to the development of the Spitfire aircraft before the War carried out vital work in the fields of aerodynamics and marine technology.

Fig. 57 *General Eisenhower. Briefing meeting in Bushy Park*

During the invasion scare of the early forties, long lines of square holes, still visible though now filled, were dug across the park, presumably to wreck any German aircraft that tried to use Bushy Park as a landing ground. Large numbers of troops were billeted on the local community and the camp included a cinema, sports pitches and a landing strip. As well as the camp, the Diana Fountain and the ponds were shrouded in camouflage netting. At its peak nearly eight thousand troops were stationed in Bushy Park.

In 1944 General Eisenhower took over part of Camp Griffiss as the Supreme Headquarters of the Allied Expeditionary Force (SHAEF). Again the old divisions of the park were respected. Camp Griffiss was erected on land which had been taken into the park after Henry VIII appropriated the village of Teddington. The northern edge of the bracken at that point marks the limit of the pre-Tudor enclosures. It was here that the Normandy invasion was planned and the chestnut blossoms that year bore silent witness to the agonising decisions which faced the Allied Forces in the last weeks of the planning process.

Towards the end of the war German and Italian prisoners of war were housed in one of the huts under the chestnut trees in the charge of the Royal Air Force. They were allowed out of the camp to work as maintenance men for the householders of Teddington and a local lending library from Twickenham was arranged for the men at the request of their chaplain.

The American camp lasted until the early 1960s. Some of the huts under the trees of Chestnut Avenue were occupied by squatters for a while, and there was agitation to keep them for temporary accommodation during the acute housing shortage. Luckily, this was resisted.

The camp was bulldozed flat, not very carefully, and there is still a great deal of concrete and other debris under the grass there which may interest future archaeologists.

A memorial was erected on the site with a dedication from the Royal Air Force to their American comrades-in-arms. It includes a quotation from Victor Hugo: 'It is through fraternity that liberty is saved.' The D-Day Commemorations in 1994 led to the re-opening of the gate into the park used by General Eisenhower now called 'Shaef Gate' and the laying of a brick pavement on the site of his office.

The National Physical Laboratory has grown to international importance over the years. Laboratories now cover Queen Adelaide's vegetable garden. The NPL is the source of measurement standards and traceability for measurement laboratories thoughout the UK and is at the forefront of technological innovation and research today. Recently, the Director has introduced an initiative to allow small groups of the public to visit Bushy House for the first time since William IV opened his door to local people on the occasion of his accession.

Bushy Park, with its gentle landscape and wide skies, is valued more greatly now than at any time. In the closing years of this millennium, there is a widespread acknowledgement that peaceful and tranquil open spaces are diminishing. Any proposal which is perceived as a threat to the essential qualities of the park is met with a fierce concerted resistance from the many thousands of people who are determined to protect the park they treasure as their own.

The great hurricane of 1987 which devastated southern England left a trail of destruction in the park. Huge giants of trees were tossed to the ground like so many spillikins. In an earlier gale in 1908, six dozen trees were lost and now the toll was much higher. The day after the storm, an eerie silence was felt by people surveying the damage. Hundreds of magnificent oaks, chestnuts and lime trees were lying on the ground as helpless as stranded ships.

During the clearing up which followed, all wood which could not be recycled was burned. The whole of that winter, the park glowed at night with the dull red heart of the fires and the air was fragrant with wood smoke. The scene had a timeless, secret atmosphere. In such a setting the images of those who have used the park over the years could spring to life. The political grandees, the royals, the Tudor schemers with their enclosures, the medieval tenant farmers and the first users of the land over four thousand years ago have all left their imprint on the grasslands of Bushy Park.

Afterword

The Royal Park of Bushy has now shifted into a higher profile as open countryside is diminishing elsewhere. Visitors value its sense of peace and tranquillity as well as its size, its wildness and its freedom. It is important to reflect that it is the responsibility of all to cherish and conserve the park for the generations to come. The wildlife, birds and trees are all part of the ecological mosaic in Bushy Park.

Wild Flowers and Trees in Bushy Park

Bushy Park is mainly of acid grassland with large areas of bracken. The anthills in the western half of the park are miniature gardens with clumps of changing forget-me-not, dove's foot cranesbill and lesser stitchwort growing there with clusters of upright chickweed and subterranean clover.

Harebell

Water Forget-me-not

The delicate blue of harebells appears in early summer. Mudwort, a nationally rare plant which flowers in July, was recognised in the boggy ground by Heron Pond in 1986. Yellow-fringed waterlilies flower on the Leg of Mutton Pond with clumps of white waterlily. Water forget-me-not, watercress and bur-marigold add colour to the ponds during summer months.

The banks of the Longford River harbour a lush profusion of water plants. Dragonflies and damsel-flies flicker in iridescent greens and blues between marsh marigold, meadowsweet and orange balsam. Over 250 plants have been recorded and the numbers are still rising.

Marsh Marigold

Nettles and thistles have their place, too. The caterpillars of several butterflies feed on these, especially those of the small tortoiseshell and red admiral butterflies. Blackberries grow in the wilder areas and autumn brings to the surface fungi including parasol mushrooms together with dangerous poisonous varieties.

Either in avenues or standing alone, in copses or in clumps, trees fill every view of Bushy Park. Two oaks south-west of the Diana Fountain are believed to date from around 1400, in which case they were already over 100 years old when the park was first enclosed.

Apart from Chestnut Avenue, most of the planting dates from the last century and the present one. Traces of avenues from the eighteenth century also remain and three of the oak trees on the north-western boundary date from the time of Henry VIII. The lime trees flower in June and have their own caterpillar, the lime hawk-moth. The newly emerged moths can be seen in the early summer evenings, flying among the branches. At twilight, the pipistrelle bats in their turn hunt above the trees. There are several bat roosts in the old trees of the park and the species recorded include daubentons (water-bats), serotines and noctules.

Hawthorn trees can be found all over the park and provide a valuable food resource for the larvae of butterflies and moths. A large variety of bird life is dependent on the haws and insects of the trees. An uncommon jewel-beetle [*Agrilus Sinatus*] has been found which breeds on the dead branches of hawthorn trees. The heady scent of red and white hawthorn blossoms fills the air each May.

The Deer and Other Animals

There are 200 fallow (male bucks and female does) and 125 red (stags and hinds) deer. The numbers are kept to the amount the land can support by culling twice a year. Great care must be taken during May, June and July when the young are born. The normally docile mothers will protec-

Red Deer

tively circle the fawns (fallow deer) and calves (red deer). They spring to the attack at any threat. They are capable of killing a dog with a blow from their sharp, pointed hooves. It is strictly forbidden to feed the deer at any time. They are undiscriminating and every year there are fatalities among them caused by ingesting plastic bags and other litter. It is the deer which are responsible for the uniform leaf line of the trees in the park.

Fallow Deer

All leaves within their height are munched off in early spring leaving a 'browse line'. In the mists of autumn, the baying of the stags resounds through the park as they lay claim to their herds. With lowered heads, the great beasts engage in fights for dominance. They move with rapier-like swiftness and can inflict serious damage to their opponent with their huge antlers.

From late October, small animals stock up with supplies of food for the winter months. Squirrels can be seen gathering nuts. Foxes, rabbits, shrews and water-voles have lived in the park for hundreds of generations.

Birds

From early spring to late summer, birdsong is the soundtrack of the park. Skylarks soar high over open spaces with a joyous tumble of song. Swallows and swifts swoop and dive, a kestrel will hover and on the ground the occasional pheasant rustles through the undergrowth.

Kestrel

Summer migrants such as spotted flycatchers and willow-warblers will add to the song of thrushes, blackbirds and robins. The kingfisher nests in the wilder areas of the park and can sometimes be spotted darting along the waterways. Winter visitors which have been recorded include siskins, stonechats, redwings and the Dartford warbler. As dusk falls, tawny owls glide through the darkening skies on their hunt for prey.

The rose-ringed parakeet is a comparative newcomer and its raucous cry can be heard from high in the treetops where it competes with starlings for nesting holes.

On the ponds and the Longford River, the still grey shadow of the heron as it stands motionless waiting for a catch is a daily event. Moorhens bob on the open waters and in spring, red-crested baby coots and striped-bodied ducklings are shepherded carefully along the sheltering banks by their mothers. They are all too vulnerable to a

Tufted Duck

hungry pike or a predatory bird such as a crow. Tufted duck and teal visit in winter. The ponds are also home to the Chinese mitten crab with its partially fur-covered pincers. It will travel over two hundred metres from the water and is increasing in numbers.

With over a hundred species of birds nesting or visiting, Bushy Park is a favourite haunt of bird watchers.

The care of Bushy Park rests with the Royal Parks Agency. A focus on conservation is now included in the management of the park.

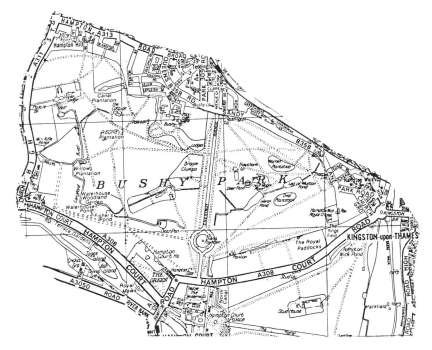

Map of Bushy Park today showing modern road systems

Illustrations

Fig. 3 *MS Cotton Julius A VI* Reproduced by permission of the Trustees of the British Museum. (© British Museum)

Figs. 4, 5, *The Luttrell Psalter* Reproduced by permission of the Trustees of the British Museum. (© British Museum)

Fig. 9 *Book of Faulconrie and Noble Art of Venerie or Hunting* George Turberville. Reproduced by permission of the Trustees of the British Library

Fig. 10 Extract. PRO: E 310/19/90

Fig. 11 *The Book of St Albans* Reproduced by permission of the Trustees of the British Museum. (© British Museum)

Figs. 13, 20, 23, 24, 25, 26, 34, 35, 37, 38 Reproduced by permission of the Trustees of the British Museum. (© British Museum)

Fig. 16 Private collection

Fig. 18 Photograph by Nicholas Bayne

Fig. 19 Reproduced by permission of the London Borough of Richmond upon Thames

Fig. 21 Extract. PRO: T 1/80

Figs. 28, 31 Reproduced by permission of the National Physical Laboratory

Fig. 36 The Royal Collection © Her Majesty The Queen

Fig. 39 Reproduced by permission of the Chatsworth Settlement Trustees

Fig. 40 Reproduced by permission of the Victoria and Albert Museum

Fig. 41 Reproduced by permission of Kingston Museum and Heritage Service

Fig. 43 Photograph (above) by Dominic White. Photograph (below) reproduced by permission of the National Trust Arlington Court Carriage Collection

Fig. 52 PRO: WORKS 16/62

Fig. 54 Photograph by Tim Davis

Line drawings by C D Freeman

Maps I–VI designed by Peter Foster. Computer graphics by the Graphic Services Department, National Physical Laboratory

Other illustrations supplied by the authors

Bibliography

Anstead, C.M. *Bushy Park – The Hanoverian Rangers* Twickenham Local History Society, 1970

Anstead, C.M. and Heath, G.D. *Bushy Park – Victorian Playground of the people* Twickenham Local History Society 1965

Camden's *Britannia,* various editions from 1695

Davies, Hunter, *A Walk round London's Parks* 1983

The Dictionary of National Biography

'E.V.B.' *Seven Gardens and a Palace* 1900

Fincham, H.W. *The Hospital of St. John of Jerusalem* 1915

Firebrace, Captain C.W. *Honest Harry, Sir Henry Firebrace* 1932

Foster, Peter *The Hospitallers at Hampton in 1338* Twickenham Local History Society 1973, 1975

Foster, Peter and Pyatt, Edward *Bushy House* 1976

Garside, Bernard *Incidents in the History of Hampton* 1937
　　　　　　The Parish Church, Rectory and Vicarage of Hampton 1937
　　　　　　The Ancient Manor Courts of Hampton 1947-9
　　　　　　The Manor Lordship and Great Parks of Hampton Court 1951

Gascoigne, Bamber and Ditchburne, Jonathan *Images of Twickenham* 1981

Greeves, Dr Tom *Bushy Park Archaeology* 1993

Heath, Gerald *Hampton Court Palace Grace and Favour in the 19th Century* Twickenham Local History Society 1988

Hopkirk, Mary *Queen Adelaide* 1946

Hutton, W.H. *Hampton Court* 1897

Jerrold, Claire *The Fair Ladies of Hampton Court* 1911

Jesse, Edward *A Summer's Day at Hampton Court* 1839
　　　　　Gleanings from Natural History 1834, 1856

Law, Ernest *The History of Hampton Court Palace* 1895-91
　　　　A Short History of Hampton Court 1906, 1929
　　　　The Chestnut Avenue 1923

Lindsay, Philip *Hampton Court* 1948

Lysons, Daniel *An Historical account of Those Parishes in the County of Middlesex which are not described in the Environs of London* 1800

Minney, R.J. *Hampton Court* 1972

Nash, Roy *Hampton Court* 1972

Norden, John *Description of Myddlesex* 1593

Orton, Margery, ed. *The Birth and Growth of Hampton Hill* 1965

Osborne, June *Hampton Court Palace* 1984

Pyatt, Edward *The National Physical Laboratory* 1983

Ripley, Henry *The History and Topography of Hampton on Thames* 1884

The Royal Parks *Bushy Park at War, D-Day* 1994
Sands, Mollie *The Gardens of Hampton Court* 1950
Selway, Neville Carr *The Regency Road* 1957
Switzer, Stephen *Introduction to Hydrostatics and Hydraulics* 1729
Tomalin, Claire *Mrs Jordan's Profession* 1994
Travers Morgan *Survey* 1992
Victoria County History of Middlesex Vols 1, 2, 3
Walford, Edward *Greater London* 1894
Yates, Edward *Hampton Court* 1935

Maps
Survey plan Hampton Court and Parks c.1709 Gough Drawing 4 fol. 62
Map of Bushy Park c. 1735 PRO: MR 1454
Survey plan of palace and both parks c.1710 PRO: WORK 32/313A
A General Plan of Hampton Court Palace Gardens and Parks signed by
Bridgeman before 1713 PRO: WORK 32/313B
Survey of the County of Middlesex 1754 by John Rocque, British Library
Environs of London 1764 by John Rocque, British Library
Plan of the Bushy Park Estate by W T Warren 1823 PRO: Work 32/653
Plan of land and premises in the parish of Hampton by E & G N Driver
1850 PRO: IR 30/21/25
Public Record Office documents include WORKS 5,6,16,19,32/ T1,
T25,T165/CRES 2,25,35

74

Index